Rumble Strip USA

Off the Interstate

Rumble Strip USA

Off the Interstate

GAIL HULNICK

WINDWORD GROUP
PUBLISHING & MEDIA

The WindWord Group
Publishing & Media
Suite 200, 100 Bull Street, Savannah, GA 31401 USA
www.windwordgroup.com

Copyright © 2019 Gail Hulnick
All Rights Reserved.

No part of this book may be scanned, reproduced or distributed in printed or electronic form without permission.

ISBN-10: 1-947527-00-2
ISBN-13: 978-1-947527-00-3

Library of Congress Control number: 2018914259

Please contact the publisher regarding large-quantity book purchases, interviews, or speaking requests
email admin@windwordgroup.com

Printed in the United States of America

DEDICATION

For the Zig, with gratitude for all the twisty roads in our life

CONTENTS

Introduction		Page	1
Chapter One	Alabama	Page	5
Chapter Two	Alaska	Page	12
Chapter Three	Arizona	Page	20
Chapter Four	California	Page	27
Chapter Five	Connecticut	Page	33
Chapter Six	Florida	Page	37
Chapter Seven	Georgia	Page	44
Chapter Eight	Idaho	Page	49
Chapter Nine	Indiana	Page	53
Chapter Ten	Kentucky	Page	57
Chapter Eleven	Louisiana	Page	68
Chapter Twelve	Maine	Page	73
Photos		Page	77
Chapter Thirteen	Massachusetts	Page	119
Chapter Fourteen	Mississippi	Page	123
Chapter Fifteen	New Hampshire	Page	129
Chapter Sixteen	New Mexico	Page	133
Chapter Seventeen	New York	Page	137
Chapter Eighteen	Ohio	Page	142
Chapter Nineteen	Rhode Island	Page	146
Chapter Twenty	South Carolina	Page	150
Chapter Twenty-One	Tennessee	Page	156
Chapter Twenty-Two	Texas	Page	159
Chapter Twenty-Three	Vermont	Page	162
Chapter Twenty-Four	Virginia	Page	167
Chapter Twenty-Five	Washington	Page	170
Playlist		Page	173
My Top Ten U.S. Drives		Page	175
About the Author		Page	176
About Rumble Strip Books		Page	177

INTRODUCTION

The American road is a thing of myth and metaphor. Taking to it, rolling along it, hypnotized by it. Tiny, twisty gravel roads through a forest, two-lane blacktop across a desert, eight-lane monsters funneling millions through a city. Choose your path and go.

For many people, that means an Interstate Highway. The Interstate system was created during the fifties and includes long, long-distance roads like I-90 and I-80, stretching about three thousand miles east to west (and vice versa) and shorter, unexpected routes like I-495 in the District of Columbia, which connects Washington DC with its suburbs in Virginia and Maryland.

Interstate highways have many advantages and beneficial features. Generally, you get there faster—higher speeds, more lanes. You get the opportunity to practice your driving skills, negotiate with big trucks, and explore all of the shopping options offered in the roadside rest stops and gas stations. You can even get a shower at the bigger ones. It's less likely you'll get lost and end up in a town where you don't know anybody and you can't find a gas station.

What they don't give is serenity or ample time for observation. By the time your companion finds the words and the pointer finger to show you something... it's gone by.

Pull off the Interstate and you discover what's really out

there. Just like in the silences during a conversation or the pauses in music, there is often more in the in-between than in the words or the notes.

Wanderlust—that urge to find out what's beyond the horizon—was not a significant part of my life all along. Other priorities and other people were more important. But I am now in a place, figuratively speaking, where travel can have its day and travel memoir can be my project.

When you write memoir, you explore epiphany. In personal memoir, it's usually an experience or another individual that causes you to change and to come to a realization. In travel memoir, it's a place or a location that causes you to open your eyes and helps you to learn something.

It would be backassward to tell you in the Introduction whether I had an epiphany or found a place that was life-changing for me. Oh, I suppose I could, and I'm not intending to play games, but I wrote the Introduction first, before all of the road trips were finished, and so I'm not done thinking about summing up. I *can* say, at this point, that if there is epiphany on these journeys, singular or plural, probably it will be light-hearted, not heavy or intense. Maybe there will be none—but maybe there will be one or more every day! In one sense, life *is* changing every day, if you're in a vehicle on a road and then sleeping in a different bed every night.

But in a less literal vein, I don't know whether truly life-changing moments will be part of this experience and this book. I suppose defining one's life as "changed" can only be done afterwards, right?

I do know that every one of these twenty-five roads was chosen to provoke thought and make a memory. Fun was also on the shopping list.

These journeys took place over four years and multiple visits to twenty-five of the United States. Some were on well-serviced, well-known secondary highways and some were on remote and much less popular byways. I looked for glimpses of history, views of everyday life, and panoramas that you couldn't find anywhere else. I also kept my nose to the ground for a sampling of regional cooking or a good story.

My traveling companion every time was the Zig, the otherwise nameless friend with the extreme driving skills and the subterranean stress level. His familiarity with America far surpasses mine, and he had many outstanding suggestions for turns to take and stops to make. His nickname is a variation on the name of a fictitious character from a British TV show, although I also think of it as half of the formula for our driving adventures.

I have been living in the U.S. for four years now. As a transplant from Canada, I found many of the customs and ideas familiar, obvious, and easy to adapt to . . . and many others, not so much. Even though the pressure to comment is certainly there, I will be giving politics the mile-wide detour and ten-foot pole they deserve in a travel memoir like this, intended to be as light-hearted as the frame of mind I cultivate. I don't feel I've yet earned the right to pass judgment or offer political opinions about places I'm passing through. I'll let you know when I'm ready.

In the meantime, let's have fun! Enjoy the thing cover-to-cover, armchair traveler–style, if you like, or sample just the region or state you happen to be passing through yourself. Mostly, the car on these trips was my red BMW 3-series convertible, although there were various rental vehicles in action a few times. The photographs are all mine.

You might know that this is the second in the *Rumble Strip* series. The rumble strip title is a reference to the line of grooves cut into pavement to make sleepy or distracted drivers smarten up and pay attention, as they drift toward the shoulder of the road (or perhaps toward a cliff that will toss them off toward a hideous death). The first book was a cross-country road trip on the Trans-Canada, in honor of that country's 150th birthday.

One of the best parts of doing the first one was compiling a music playlist for readers to use, while daydreaming or actually traveling. I supplied the titles, singers, bands and writers behind 150 Canadian tunes and put it up on the online music-sharing site Spotify. At the end of this book you'll find songs, for you to use as companions during your exploration of each of the twenty-five states featured in Rumble Strip USA off the Interstate.

Yes, I know there are fifty and we still have some more driving to do. Actually, not that much driving, just a lot of writing. I have been to forty-nine of the fifty states. The quirkiest part of the numbers is that the forty-ninth one I saw, after this whole project began in 2014, was Alaska—the forty-ninth one to join the United States (in 1959, although the U.S. bought it in 1867).

From Russia.

For $7,200,000.

The book is organized alphabetically, beginning with Alabama and ending with Washington. It covers road trips in precisely half of the United States, with a toe dipped in the water of every region. The exploration began in 2014, but most of the drives took place in 2017 and 2018.

Oh—which one is still missing? It's a trip to Nebraska that is still on the horizon rather than in the bag.

So, buckle up, pull out whichever road snacks you like, and put it in gear. You see that next exit sign on the Interstate? We're pulling off to explore some side roads.

Chapter One

ALABAMA

My trip through Alabama came about because of Hurricane Irma. Living in Coastal Georgia, and having been through Hurricane Matthew in October of 2016 (warm-up provided by Tropical Storm Hermine on Labor Day weekend in 2016), I should have been better prepared and aware when the watches and warnings started flowing in September 2017. But hurricane prediction is not an exact science. In the early part of a late summer month that delivered not just Irma but Hurricane Maria too, it was very difficult to get a fix on what was happening and what to do.

But as the days went by and the path of the storms became clearer, the decisions got easier to make. When the mandatory evacuation notice came for Savannah, my first plan was to head north and inland. The trip started with a destination of Birmingham, Alabama. Hurricane Irma changed direction and speed a few times and eventually, the itinerary shifted to include miles farther north, up to Memphis, then a swing west and south through Mississippi down to New Orleans, with a final leg east along the Gulf Coast to northern Florida, where we encountered numerous vehicles filled with families displaced by the storm.

Hurricane Irma cost us a few trees and shingles but no

significant damage—nothing even remotely close to the devastation suffered in some communities from Hurricanes Harvey, Irma, Katie, José, and Maria, in the summer of 2017, one of the worst on record for Atlantic storms.

But like thousands of others, we had some days of anxiety, far away from home and not sure what was happening there or what we'd find when we returned.

As we headed into the state I was thinking, "Alabama, you'll have to be *very* interesting to distract me from what's going on—or might be going on—at home in Georgia."

And it was. The Zig and I explored Birmingham a bit, listing many places we'd like to return to: the Civil Rights District, the Barber Vintage Motorsports Museum, the Alabama Theatre.

Hurricane Irma's path had turned westward now and the bad weather was heading for Birmingham. We needed to move on.

I have to confess that I had stereotypes and expectations about each of the states we traveled through. How could you not, given the tidal wave of books, movies, and TV shows there are and have been over decades (even a century!) of production by American writers, both resident and visiting. I don't want to spend a lot of time in this book exploring those preconceptions, because I want the focus to be on the present, on what I was actually learning, rather than fearing because of some old movie. But in the spots where those notions were exploded or even gently rocked, I'll point them out. And in the spots where I noticed they were confirmed, I'll mention that too.

In Alabama, as expected, the weather was hot and the people were soft-spoken and friendly.

I picked I-65 to use going north and then near Decatur we turned off on Highway 72, heading west toward Florence. I had three stops in mind for this region in the northwest corner of Alabama, all of them birthplaces: Helen Keller's at Tuscumbia, W.C. Handy's in Florence, and the Muscle Shoals Sound Studio, the place where Bob Dylan's "Gotta Serve

Somebody" and Paul Simon's "Kodachrome" were born on vinyl.

A surprise architectural star was a bonus.

Ivy Green is the name of the farm in Tuscumbia built by Helen Keller's grandfather decades ago. If you're not familiar with her story and you like movies, take a look at *The Miracle Worker*, produced several times for film and television. Probably the best-known version stars Anne Bancroft and Patty Duke, and if you are a teacher or have any teachers in your family, it will probably make you all weep. It's the story of Helen's teacher, Anne Sullivan, as much as it is the story of Helen's triumph. Helen's life story has been told many times, as far back as a silent film in 1919.

Helen contracted a disease in childhood that left her unable to see or hear. After many years unable to speak, as a result of Anne Sullivan's efforts Helen learns to use her voice. The scene in the play and in the movie when Anne uses a water pump to teach Helen to make the connection between a thing, its name, and the way to say it is incredible. The scene is memorialized in the garden behind Helen's childhood home in a statue of Helen and Anne in that moment.

Helen moved with her teacher to New York to continue her education. She went to Radcliffe College in 1900 and was the first deaf-blind person to earn a Bachelor of Arts degree. She went on to write and publish books, give public lectures, and help in the founding of the American Civil Liberties Union in the 1920s. She was and is an inspiration for foundations and institutes for the blind in dozens of countries around the world. Streets have been named after her in countries including the United States, India, Spain, and Israel. Stamps and coins have been issued in her honor, with the state of Alabama's quarter featuring Braille language on the coin.

We drove up to a white house on a large lot in West Tuscumbia, Alabama, on a sunny afternoon. Some sort of event was just ending. I found out later it was a gathering of local supporters of the Lion's Club. Service organizations and institutes for the blind and the visually impaired around the world treasure this place because of Helen's work throughout her lifetime on their behalf.

The house was built in 1820 and survived the Civil War. It's on the National Register of Historic Places and is maintained down to the smallest detail. The grounds are worth a visit all on their own for any landscaper or lover of gardens, with magnolias, mimosas, English ivy, and a canopy of boxwood trees more than 150 years old.

Helen's books and her speeches exude optimism, joy, curiosity, and imagination. She has always been one of my heroes and having some time to walk around the place where she began her amazing life was so memorable. I had no idea she was born in Alabama nor that people in the state had done so much to honor her memory.

My next two destinations had to do with music. Blues pioneer W.C. Handy is revered all over Memphis and Beale Street, where he moved in his mid-thirties, and he lived and worked in many other southern states during his twenties. But it is Florence, Alabama that claims the "Father of the Blues" as a native son. The small cabin where he was born in 1873 and where he spent his early years has been preserved as a museum.

We pulled into the outside lot at five minutes to four in the afternoon, with the posted closing time shown as four p.m. We parked the car and went up to the entrance. I really thought we'd be out of luck. However, a very friendly young man held the door open for us, gave us tickets, and left us to wander through rooms filled with W.C. Handy's personal papers and memorabilia. The highlight for me was the piano where he composed "St. Louis Blues".

Beside the museum and the library, you can see the two rooms of the cabin where he grew up, preserved and equipped as they might have been in the 1870s.

The next stop on my Alabama highlights reel was a building on a very quiet street corner in Sheffield. This was the home of Muscle Shoals Sound Studio, which since its founding has been the birthplace for albums made by a remarkable list of recording artists. This next list goes on a while, but I hope you'll forgive me. Some of my all-time favorite music is here: "Wild Horses" from the Rolling Stones. The Staple Singers' "I'll Take You There". Bob Seger's "Old Time Rock and Roll", and two years earlier, "Night Moves". Boz Scaggs's *Boz Scaggs*. Rod Stewart's *Atlantic Crossing*. Dr. Hook recorded half a dozen albums here and Lynyrd Skynyrd did *Skynyrd's First: The Complete Muscle Shoals Album*. Cher is given credit as recording the first album at the studio, in 1969— her sixth, *3614 Jackson Highway* (which is the street address of the studio). Aretha Franklin, Glenn Frey, Wilson Pickett, Willie Nelson, Levon Helm, Leon Russell, Cat Stevens, and Joe Cocker all walked up to this door, at one time or another.

After a move to a different building in the late seventies and then a move back, followed by a listing on the National Register of Historic Places and a documentary that rekindled interest in the history of this corner of Alabama, the tide of interest in Muscle Shoals was rising. Apparently a large donation (reportedly a million dollars) from Beats Electronics made the preservation possible.

I have to confess that although I'd heard the term "the muscle shoals sound" before, I wasn't too clear on what it was, where it came from, or how it was spelled. Turns out it was essentially the product of a tight group of the best studio musicians around, The Muscle Shoals Rhythm Section, known affectionately as "The Swampers". They owned the studio and the publishing and production companies associated with it. Some of the interviews about the time say that the term just arose because some of the people involved began using it in imitation of references to the "Motown sound", the "Nashville sound", the "Memphis sound". The city became a magnet for musicians from around the world, and at its peak there were eight studios in the region. People just thought it was a place to find the best musicians and the funkiest sound and that it had a lot more soul than New York or L.A.

It's hard to imagine the scene of the time, if you think of those bold-face names as famous stars. You have to wonder where they stayed, ate, took a break. The neighborhood was basic and about as far from the bright–lights, big–city scene as you could get. But when you think of them as hard-working musicians, trying to achieve top quality songs that would express their own heart and touch others, you can imagine that the low-key vibe of the place and its remoteness from New York or L.A. wouldn't matter. They came here and they recorded riffs and lyrics that would settle into the DNA of a generation.

The fourth stop in this northwest corner of Alabama, just off Highway 72 in Florence, was the Frank Lloyd Wright Rosenbaum House—the architectural gem referred to previously. It's the only house designed by Wright in the southeast that is open to the public (at this time) and is one of the few in that region at all. When you come around the curve on Riverview Drive, it's a bit startling to see it there, in the midst of the more traditional residences in the neighborhood, and in the state as a whole. Maybe even the whole South. Columns, verandas, second and third stories—you'll see enough of those to fill your bucket till Easter. But you won't see much contemporary—until you see this. And it is an outstanding exception. It's long, low, and modern; it was intended as a lower-cost alternative for middle-income families. Lower cost, perhaps, but upper style, in my opinion. Not just mine—many others put it right up there with Wright's masterpieces Fallingwater and Taliesin West.

Although it is open to the public, we weren't driving by during the hours when we could have toured. But I enjoyed seeing the exterior. A look at the website shows that the interior features long, low horizontal lines, floor to ceiling glass, dark enclosed hallways and other spaces that open up into airy, uplifting rooms. A house that would have been a thrill to live in.

Our stay in Alabama ended with a northward turn to Tennessee, heading for Memphis as shelter from the storm. A drive from the birthplace of Helen Keller and W.C. Handy to the birthplace of rock 'n' roll—a natural progression, yes? The Hurricane Irma evacuation road trip eventually took us from

Memphis to Highway 61 through Mississippi to New Orleans and then east along the Gulf coast to Florida and then north, back to Savannah. From the Yellowhammer state to the Volunteer state to the Magnolia state to the Mardi Gras state and home to the Peach state.

Who was it who came up with the idea of giving nicknames to states, anyway? And which one was the first? I don't know, but I do have an opinion about which one probably has the most.

Chapter Two

ALASKA

Alaska is the state that probably has more nicknames than most of the others.

Actually, I don't know that for sure and I wouldn't bet money on it. It would be fun to run a contest, maybe. Anyway, Alaska has quite a few. *The Last Frontier. The Great Alone. The Land of the Midnight Sun.* I should specify, too, that I'm talking about well-known nicknames, the ones that pop up as soon as you mention a name like Texas or Alaska. Organic, deeply rooted nicknames. Not those awkward slogans or taglines, recently printed on a poster or pressed into a license plate, written by some official committee. Real nicknames.

I didn't go very far into The Great Alone and I certainly wasn't near any Last Frontier. (Is there even one of those left on the globe?) I also didn't see it during the Midnight Sun weeks in the summer. It was a short visit in March, when the snow was still flying, the temperature falling, and the days ending early. We started in Anchorage and went to the east, off the Interstate.

This raises the interesting question of whether, by definition, you can have an "Interstate" in Alaska. Or Hawaii.

As I mentioned in the Introduction, Alaska is the forty-ninth state I've visited, and coincidentally, the forty-ninth state to join the United States. It's the farthest north and farthest west I've been (although that's a bit of a theoretical concept, when you're talking about a globe. Depends which direction you're facing, I suppose). It's certainly one of the most exotic places in the world, in my mind and perhaps in yours, too. Distant, lightly populated, extreme climate, difficult to access at certain times, home to many hardy, unusual people with unique stories.

We visited March 1st to 5th, 2018. As we flew in to Anchorage, I could see Cook Inlet, ice chunks floating in it. Mountains covered in miles of snow stretched out below, vertically and horizontally, with glaciers sliding into the water. As we got closer to the airport and came in to land, I could see massive cargo planes, with Cathay Pacific logos, parked near the terminals. Alaska is the biggest stop for planes from China and other countries of the Pacific Rim. It's not that far, really, if you consider the curvature of the globe.

When I walked out of the airport in Anchorage the cold stopped me, cold. I had been in cold places before—I spent my childhood in Canadian cities, Edmonton, Winnipeg, and Toronto, and I worked as a TV news reporter, visiting small communities in the north. But this was unlike any cold I'd felt before. Maybe my physical tolerance had changed, after living three and a half years in the southern U.S. or maybe my clothes were all wrong. Whatever. It was cold. Which way to the French onion soup and the brandy?

Driving is challenging in any place with snow and ice. Within ten minutes of leaving the airport in our rented Ford Explorer, I saw a woman in a four-wheel drive vehicle perched on top of a snow drift about three feet up, facing the wrong way. How did she get there and how would she get down? She was holding a cellphone to her ear so it was a pretty good bet that help was on the way. The climate in Alaska would have been a lot more of an issue in pre-cellphone days.

This was to be a very brief road trip. Another time (the

next time?) I want to explore much farther. I'd also like to return to see Alaska in summer. But for this time we had planned a forty-mile drive in snowy conditions east of Anchorage along the Seward Highway to Alyeska, a winter sports resort, and to the Alaska Wildlife Conservation Center at Girdwood. The first stop of the day, though, was a park near downtown Anchorage that was just a few miles from the start of the Iditarod.

The Iditarod is one of the premiere athletic events, right up there with the Super Bowl, the World Cup or the Kentucky Derby, in my opinion. It's one of the most demanding sled dog races in the world, requiring mushers to spend days and days outdoors on a trail, guiding, motivating, and caring for a team of incredible dog-athletes. And guiding, motivating, and caring for themselves.

It was a complete fluke that I was there the same weekend as the race. I stood with about two dozen others at a bend in the trail in the woods near Alaska Pacific University, up to mid-calf in powder snow, fingers rigid as popsicles, hair icing up after getting damp from the exertion of walking in to this vantage point. Imagine life as an Iditarod competitor—weeks of preparation; raising the entry fee; gathering supplies and dog food for caches at stopping points along the thousand-mile trail; preparing the dogs and yourself to survive an eight-to-ten day journey across Alaska, from Anchorage to Nome. Take the slight discomfort I felt from cold fingers, icy hair, achingly cold feet in boots with no lining, and shivers due to the wind blowing through my silly coat . . . and then multiply it ten-fold. Twenty, maybe. Long stretches of solitude ahead on the trail, nights lonely and dark. Dangers such as sleds turning over, ice breaking under the runners, the musher tangling in reins and pulled along by dogs that won't stop.

But . . . looking at it another way, the temperature was only 24 degrees, not minus 45. There was no blizzard, just a chance of snow, sky a clear, bright blue. There would be a full moon tonight. The men and women running these teams knew there was risk, as there is in every sport, and that, for them, it was outweighed.

And looking at it yet another way, for me, the sight of those teams zooming around the curve in the trail, sleds skimming along snow so white, mushers in colorful parkas and boots, riders beaming with the thrill of it, and dogs with paws protected by booties and eyes blazing with eagerness to run—well, it's a thrill I won't forget.

Seeing the Iditarod was something that had been on the loosely defined dream trips list I'd been carrying around for a million years. Arriving in Anchorage on the eve of the ceremonial start of the 46th running of this thousand-mile race was completely coincidental but was definitely one of those opportunities to leap on.

My interest in the race went back more than thirty years. I first met Susan Butcher, one of the pioneers—and champions—of the race in the eighties when I was hosting a radio talk show in Edmonton, Alberta, and I'd never forgotten her. Susan was an energetic woman with dark hair in a long braid, a wide smile, and eyes that were full of joy. We were interviewing her because she was on tour as the second woman to win the Iditarod; later she became the first person to win four out of five consecutive races. She was born near Boston and went to Alaska as a twenty-year-old, drawn by the call of the wilderness. She started out with only two dogs and eventually became a champion.

Her many achievements as an athlete include setting speed records for the Iditarod throughout the eighties and nineties. She was an ambassador for the sport until her passing in 2006. The first Saturday in March each year in Alaska is Susan Butcher Day.

The ceremonial start was in downtown Anchorage and the excitement was huge. You can get up quite close to the mushers and the dogs and watch them get ready. There was also a carnival, ice sculptures, and something called the "Running of the Reindeer". This involves people in costumes running down the main street ahead of a herd of reindeer. Think Pamplona and the bulls, but with a wider street, smaller animals, and a much lower danger element. Yes, a reindeer does have a rack of antlers that could be harmful if brandished the wrong way but somehow an animal that has such connections with Santa Claus doesn't transmit much menace. The runners all seemed to be laughing and having a good time, which is never the impression I've had when I've watched the Spanish version on TV.

The next day, about seventy miles down the road at Willow, the official start of the Iditarod takes place. This is the serious business, the real deal. The prize money this year was $580,000 (down somewhat from previous years) and that's divided among the top thirty finishers.

And finishing is an issue, by the way. Every year there are teams, some of them champions from previous years, who have to pull out along the way. Injuries, supply problems, team trouble, lead dog trouble, too many 'dropped dogs' (those who are injured or ill and are left behind to be picked up and shipped home), weather disasters—there are many reasons. The winner is supposed to get $75,000 and then the size of the prize declines from there, depending on where the team ends up in the ranking. If you finish at all, you get $1,000.

The entry fee this year was $4,000, so essentially you are paying to be there.

Most of the mushers aren't in it for the money, anyway, I would guess. It's the prestige, the experience, the sport, and the personal challenge. But just in case you're thinking "Cool, I'll add this to my bucket list, right up there behind 'climbing Diamond Head' or 'riding a horse in the Andes'—", they tell me it costs about $30,000 to take part. The top contenders have kennels with eighty dogs in them, and do many other races, in places like Yukon and Norway.

Sixty-seven mushers, down five or six from last year, started out on the 2018 Iditarod, seventeen of them women. After we'd seen about thirty of the teams go by, I could feel the Zig's interest dropping off, and even I had to concede that the dogs were starting to look a lot alike. We hiked back up the snowy hill to the rental car and set out for the drive to Alyeska.

As I mentioned, the vehicle was a Ford Explorer—a nice choice for winter roads.

The route takes you south from Anchorage along Seward Highway to Turnagain Arm, which the encyclopedia tells me is noteworthy for having the second highest tides in North America, after the Bay of Fundy. Seward was the U.S. Treasury Secretary in 1867 who organized the buying of Alaska from Russia. The name comes from the time of the first European visitors and Captain Cook's explorations, with reports of voyages that involved "turn" and then "turn again" commands.

This highway is one of the most scenic in the U.S. and has been included in a list of only thirty or so drives designated by a Congressional program as an All-American Road, within the larger category of National Scenic Byways. The views were spectacular, with the wide flats of Turnagain Arm on the right, stretching to the opposite shores of Cook Inlet, and on the left the Chugach Mountains.

This area is fascinating to students of Alaska history, not only because of the European exploration in the eighteenth century, the Russian connection through the nineteenth century, and the Gold Rush late in that century, but also because of geological history.

Earthquakes are numerous in Alaska—about five thousand a year. In 1964, in an area about seventy-eight miles east of Anchorage in Prince William Sound, the biggest earthquake in North American history measured 9.2 on the Richter scale. You can still see some of the impact in downtown Anchorage where streets buckled and buildings shifted in landslides. Hundreds of people died in related tsunamis. You can research the event in great detail by visiting Earthquake Park in Anchorage.

The weather conditions that day supplied me with the other of the two possibilities in March—blowing snow (and bitter cold). Not many other vehicles were out on the road, but perhaps not many others had just one day to take a sip of Alaska. Even though obscured a bit, I had amazing views of the Chugach Mountain range and Captain Cook Inlet, with chunks of ice floating in a current strong enough to see.

We pulled in at the Alaska Wildlife Conservation Center and happily paid the $15 each to support the efforts of this place to extend the survival of these animals on the planet. Many of those housed here were brought in orphaned or injured. Most people, like us, will never get another opportunity to see them so close up. And yes, why should we, and yes, I do know the arguments against zoos or enclosures of any kind. But I still think the educational benefits are not to be discounted, and this education is happening under controlled circumstances with just a few animals, relatively speaking, and on a 1.5-mile loop in relatively close proximity to a major city. The center allows people to see these wild animals without traveling out into the core of their natural habitat, disrupting it with jeeps or tour buses—or, even worse, hunting rifles.

Moose, lynx, bison, bear, deer, eagles, elk, foxes, musk ox, owls, porcupines, wolves, and reindeer. That's what we saw that Saturday in March. We bundled up and headed out to walk around their enclosures and see a few things we'd only previously seen in books, online or on screen. A few rhetorical and random questions I had when I left: Does a moose like to be indoors, out of the elements? Why does a full-grown lynx somehow look as though it's an adolescent one? Can a bison run fast, with those legs? Why don't bears like to live in herds? Could a deer be trained to ignore headlights? Does an eagle have any sense of how majestic it seems? Is an elk bigger or smaller than a mountain goat? Do the foxes really stay here or do they just shimmy under whatever fence and go wherever they want? What's the origin of the word 'musk' in the name 'musk ox'? Why did J.K. Rowling choose owls? Why do do some people think it is pronounced pork-ee-pine? Are wolves as dangerous as the movies make them out to be? Could people run with the reindeer the way they run with the bulls in Pamplona?

The next transition was a jarring one—from the freezing

cold environment of wild animals to a cozy restaurant at Alyeska Resort. Alaska is the frontier but it also has many elements of American comfort and first-world ease. This resort offers everything the winter sports crowd is seeking, with many dining options, too. We had lunch at the Sakura Restaurant, one of many experiences on the west and northern coasts that will remind you that you are part of the Pacific Rim. The skiing and riding, they tell me, are exceptional, and the nickname for the mountain is "steep and deep".

We returned that evening to Anchorage, our brief visit to Alaska almost at an end. The city seemed to be full of friendly people, many of them locals but many others from out of town. We went for drinks and a light dinner in a restaurant downtown and ended up visiting and discussing the menu with people at the tables all around, some from other parts of Alaska, some international and in town for the dog race, and some from Oregon and in town for a college basketball final.

Liquor licensing is an entertaining topic, in many places. There is no end to the variations on "we have rules to make sure we're protected from your inability to monitor your own intake and behave like a grown-up." On another night out, we found that the liquor license allowed food in the restaurant but not in the bar, but permitted alcohol in the bar and no wine or beer or anything else alcoholic on the menu in the restaurant. As you might expect, the bar was packed and the restaurant had two people.

That night I was back at the airport, waiting for a night flight back to Atlanta. My next trip to Alaska will have to include a foray to Denali, the continent's highest peak. From high to low— one of my stops in the next state took in one of the continent's lowest points.

Chapter Three

ARIZONA

From the highest peak to one of the deepest canyons. Millions of people visit Arizona to see the Grand Canyon, one of the natural wonders of the world, and I had that sight high on my list. It happened by accident that the night I was there was the night of a lunar eclipse of a 'supermoon', a lifetime memory even for a person not usually a knowledgeable or frequent sky-watcher.

We crossed into Arizona after driving over from California, and passing through Needles, one of the hottest places I've ever been. *One hundred eleven degrees!* read the gauge on the dashboard (the exclamation mark is mine, though. I'm still waiting for the car that puts one of those on its speedometer readings.) Given the way my skin felt, I could certainly believe the temperature was that high in Needles, an appropriately named city.. The top on the car *was* down when we started the day's road trip, but after a while it just had to go up.

At the border, we turned north on Route 66, also called the Mother Road, the Will Rogers Highway, and the Main Street of America. It has some incredible stretches through

Arizona and we decided to make that the focus of this off-the-Interstate trip. That, and the Grand Canyon of course. Route 66 was one of the original highways in the American system, established in 1926. It runs from Chicago to Los Angeles, with its terminus at the Santa Monica Pier. It was the highway that John Steinbeck's Okies used to flee from the dustbowl conditions of the thirties. It was the highway romanticized by Jack Kerouac and the Beat poets. It's a two-lane road, running 2,448 miles, with about four hundred of them in Arizona.

Although it was decommissioned in the mid-eighties, large sections of Route 66 are still navigable. Particularly on the stretch east of Flagstaff, the old towns, neon signs, motels and gas station buildings from the twenties and thirties have been preserved. The highway was celebrated and referenced in pop culture through songs urging listeners to get their kicks on Route 66, TV shows following a Corvette and its owners' adventures, films featuring easy motorcycle riders, and animated movies showcasing talking cars. Today, it's all very kitschy, with a Route 66 passport and gift stores all over the place, but it's still fun.

This area west of Flagstaff begins with the northward turn up toward Oatman. The drive was a bit nerve-racking for me, reminding me of the cliff-cuddling experience of the Cabot Trail in Nova Scotia. When you're the passenger, you see the great beyond down below much more clearly than the driver does; he or she (ideally) is concentrating on the road and the other vehicles. Luckily for me, the Zig is an outstanding driver and I never once had to scream out loud. But really, the sight of a long, sheer slope, down to a dry, desert floor thousands of feet below, was enough to make me crave a return to the Interstate. But if we'd backtracked we would have missed one of the other most memorable aspects of Route 66 through Arizona.

In Oatman, a lot of the inhabitants walk on four legs. These burros, apparently, have been there since the early twentieth century (no, of course not these particular individuals). The burros are descendants of pack animals turned loose by the gold prospectors between 1915 and 1924. They stand quietly along the sides of the main street, ready for their close-up as tourists pose for selfies. They are gentle, but they are wild, and signs warn tourists to be cautious around them.

Another part of the history of Oatman is that movie stars Clark Gable and Carole Lombard honeymooned here in 1939, after getting married in Kingman. Gable fell in love with the area and often returned to play poker with the miners. Their honeymoon suite is one of the town's attractions, as is the story of a ghost inhabiting the hotel.

I couldn't help but notice that Oatman is very proud of its connection with Route 66 and there are almost as many tourist souvenirs related to the Mother Road as there are in Winslow, Arizona, farther east down the road, past Flagstaff.

I finished staring at the burros and resisting the urge to acquire one more piece of paraphernalia with "66" on it, and climbed into the car to push on to Kingman.

East and west of Kingman, we found one of the longest remaining stretches of Route 66—158 miles of very old road. For the benefit of the car and my tush, I wanted to take it very slowly. If you have a zippy little sports car and you like to open it up, this is not the side road for you.

Wildflower photographers are in heaven on this section of the road. The flowers start to bloom in February and continue through May, according to the clerk at the gas station, and if you love scenes of colorful flowers against a desert landscape, this is the place.

The fifty-two miles between Kingman and Topock, on the Colorado River, are part of the original Mother Road. It was carved out even earlier than 1926, to provide a route for those prospectors trying to make their fortunes during the Oatman Gold Rush. This is what the road west looked like to the people John Steinbeck depicted in the *Grapes of Wrath*. Five decades later, the road was being upgraded and linked to I-40, to adapt to bigger vehicles.

At Seligman you can reconnect with I-40 if you crave an

Interstate experience for a while. That's what we did, although it wasn't craving an Interstate experience so much as having a desire to get there faster. We followed the highway into Flagstaff, then turned north toward the Grand Canyon on Highway 64.

I don't know what it is that is so compelling about the Grand Canyon. It's not the deepest or the widest one. The weather can be very unpredictable; I remembered that on my first visit there a fall storm had poured clouds and mists into the canyon and you couldn't even tell it was there. I was seriously unimpressed, I have to tell you—to the point where making a return visit wasn't on my radar at all.

I was happy that I had changed my mind. This time, in very early fall, the skies were clear and my first views of the canyon were every bit as spectacular as I'd been led to believe. The depths of it aren't what appealed to me, particularly. It was the color, the stripes of gold, pink, orange, black. I can't even begin to do justice to it, with words, and most of the photographs I've seen don't either.

As I mentioned, I was there, coincidentally, on the day of the lunar eclipse of a 'supermoon', with the bodies in orbit passing unusually close to each other and the view from many places on earth correspondingly breathtaking.

The approach to the Grand Canyon is actually kind of low-key; I'd seen more anticipation, thanks to numerous billboards, for a Mexican-themed roadside attraction in South Carolina than for this wonder of the world. Parking was easy, the stroll in to the viewing area also low-stress. It wasn't horrendously crowded but as the sun set and the darkness started to descend, the foot-traffic picked up. By moonrise time, people were shoulder to shoulder at the railings.

"Where are you from?" I asked a woman whose British accent I'd picked up beside me while I was scanning the horizon with binoculars.

"Liverpool," she said. "Bloody amazing, isn't it?"

Since we were here to watch a blood moon, which is another way of saying a total lunar eclipse, that was a good adjective.

"Munich, for us," said another person at the railing. "You?"

"Right here in the U.S.," I said. "You've traveled a long way."

"We have some amazing sights, too," she said. "You should plan a trip or two our way."

"A lot of the good places are just overrun now," the first woman added. Nods of agreement from either side of us.

It's difficult to take an opinion on this issue of over tourism. Yes, the sights and attractions need the numbers of visitors, to pay wages and give jobs to the local people, even to keep going, in some cases, where maintenance costs are significant. But when the number of people visiting climbs so high that the local flavor is completely lost, when locals can barely get on their own public transit, when even a registration system and limiting visitor numbers doesn't seem to work—you realize there has to be a balance. The main concern is for the local residents, in my opinion, but there's also the point of view of the tourist to be considered. I remember visiting Stonehenge—pumped to wander around the ancient, mysterious structures imagining Druids and portals for time travel—and being absolutely stunned by the numbers of people, busloads and busloads of them arriving. Not that I think mystical, historic places need to be kept pristine and authentic just for my benefit; I'm just one tourist of the millions. But I won't go back and I don't recommend a visit to Stonehenge to anybody.

The lunar eclipse was beginning and the hum of conversation among the tourists was gone. Slowly, almost elegantly, the dark shadow of the earth began to cover the moon. It was a bit like watching paint dry, but compelling, nonetheless. About half the way through, though, people began to leave for their cars. I saw that a few smart ones had flashlights, and that would definitely help for the return walk to the parking lot.

Leave early or stay until the last minutes before totality?

We split the difference and walked back to the car when there was still a bit of moonlight to use to see the path, then sat on the hood and watched the last minutes of the eclipse.

Next morning I was anxious to get going to see Winslow. The road from the Grand Canyon back to the Interstate was probably a bit busier than usual, with all those eclipse tourists on it, but it was still a pleasant drive. We jumped off I-40 east of Flagstaff, onto Route 66 again. This stretch is like the scene from any movie about the iconic road, especially that cute little animated one, *Cars*. Diners, gas stations, motels. Then about fifty-eight miles east of Flagstaff you roll up into Winslow. I love the Eagles song "Take it Easy", and apparently I'm not the only one. The girl in the flatbed Ford is there, illustrated in what might be called, loosely, sculpture. The corner is certainly there, and the logo 66 is painted at the junction, right in the middle of town. A souvenir store provides pretty much every sort of take-home item you might want, and while I drew the line at the neon-colored burros, the decals, and the miniature cactus, I did leave with a T-shirt.

The weather had moderated and Needles was (were?) a distant memory now. Arizona temperatures can top three figures easily and often, through the summer and fall months, but early October can be unpredictable, too. This time, it was beautiful and the next part of the road trip, through the Painted Desert, couldn't have been designed to be more perfect. The Painted Desert, named for its blazing colors, is in the northern part of Petrified Forest National Park. About half the park is wilderness and the hiking is phenomenal; you see trees that are 225 million years old.

The Painted Desert extends northward into Navajo country. If going off-road appeals to you, get a permit, then enjoy!

Arizona has inspired many songwriters, with references to a specific place, to a city, or to the state as a whole, or to a relationship, an experience or a dream. The roads themselves have also been a prompt to some lyricists, with a carefree highway and a route to get your kicks. It would be an interesting discussion sometime, to debate which state has been more of an inspiration: Arizona? Or this next one, where it never rains?

Chapter Four

CALIFORNIA

Maybe it never rains, or maybe it pours, but not on the weekend we drove the California road I chose for this collection. The route runs between Los Angeles and Palm Springs, a popular destination for decades and a place you can reach from the City of Angels in one hour thirty-seven minutes on I-10.

Instead, this time, my route was Highway 60 and the plan was to do a circle, starting at LAX, driving north to 60 and then east to Palm Springs, on day one. We would be in the desert overnight for a special event, then back on 74, go west to I-5, and then north back to the airport to drop off the rental car and get on a plane home to the East Coast.

It was tough to pick a California road for this book since I've been all over the state many times, and there are so many spectacular drives. Highway 1, along the Pacific Coast. The Silverado Trail, through Napa Valley. Highway 120 through Yosemite National Park. The Redwood Highway, Highway 101. The 17-Mile Drive on the Monterey Peninsula. And that's just for starters. How did I choose? With a blindfold and a dart pointed at a wall map. (Maybe eventually there will have to be a Rumble Strip California.) There was one other factor—a concert I wanted to see in Palm Springs, with the legendary Van Morrison doing one of only a handful of concerts that year in the U.S.

At the airport, when you say you are going to Palm Springs, people inevitably say, "Are you going to golf?"

No! There are other things to do there, you know. Hiking, camping, swimming, dining, sight-seeing, just plain enjoying life. All in a climate that is a bit warm in summer but very welcome when you're arriving from anywhere with too much snow or too few degrees above freezing.

The folks at the rental car office were friendly and, it turned out, generous. Somehow, with no extra bucks of our own, the Zig and I were being upgraded to a Mercedes two-seater with a retractable convertible roof. Many firsts on this trip: I had never ridden in a car like this, and I had never driven through the desert on side roads like 60 and 74.

The first stage, near Los Angeles through the dense suburb of Culver City, had us on freeways with five lanes going in each direction. The hills were dry and brown on this October day and at times, through the haze, they were just blurred shapes. The vegetation consisted mainly of shrubs with reddish, purple, and pink flowers, although I did see a few palm trees. It was 83 degrees just before 11 a.m. but I could feel that it would be even hotter before the sun set that night.

Just before we reached San Jacinte the freeway changed to two lanes in each direction, with fewer bumps and holes in the pot. I could see bigger hills and, overall, things felt just not quite as dry. The next eight miles, to Beaumont, gave us a twisty road, always appreciated, even if it was mainly uphill, as this one was. In the last twenty-eight miles to Palm Springs, I saw wind farms by the thousands, billboards every quarter mile, a lot of sand near the shoulders, and a thermometer that read 97 degrees.

Palm Springs is actually four cities: Palm Springs, Desert Springs, Rancho Mirage, and Palm Desert. You have Cathedral City in there, too. Roads and streets are named for famous performers from the fifties and sixties who had homes there and liked to leave work behind in L.A. while they came out to the desert to party. Frank Sinatra, Dinah Shore, and Bob Hope are memorialized on the street signs, along with a few politicians such as Gerald Ford.

We passed many golf courses. I later researched and learned there are more than seventy! How do they keep them all so green in a place with so little water?

The architecture features a lot of low-rise, flat-roofed, contemporary-style buildings, with adobe, sand, and gray the colors of choice. The high-rise resorts go seven or eight stories, many with casinos attached. As it's been for decades, Palm Springs is a place people go to party and to relax. In the first group, you find a lot of wedding tourism, both for destination weddings and bachelor and bachelorette parties, and in the second group, a lot of 'snowbirds', many of them in recreational vehicles, fleeing the northern climate.

On the weekend we were there Palm Springs seemed to be hosting a lot of bachelors and bachelorettes soon to relinquish that status. In our hotel I saw something I'd not seen before at this sort of resort in this sort of place—security guards. I asked a server why and she said some of the bachelors and bachelorettes have too much to drink and need an authoritative escort back to their rooms to settle down for a while.

The concert was at the Agua Caliente Resort on Bob Hope Drive in Rancho Mirage. It was a smallish room and the sightlines were fantastic. The concert was forty-five minutes, tight and short, and maybe from a different performer it might have seemed brief. But five minutes of Van Morrison is worth fifty minutes of anybody else, so it was just terrific. He opened with "Moondance" and closed with "Gloria". Song after song, hit after hit, sensational. He doesn't talk to the audience or spend any time putting a song into context. The band had to change instruments, tune up, and sync in a matter of seconds, in some cases; he definitely had them on their toes.

Van Morrison is an amazing performer for someone more

than seventy years old—he would be, for any age! The experience went well for some people and not for others. To the left of me, I overheard "Why aren't more people dancing in their seats? You and I did. I don't see how people can sit still!" and to the right, "Why didn't he play more of the old stuff? That was just boring."

I saw many people who looked like older musicians, with long hair, black clothing, a lot of jewelry and an overall vibe that was stylish and cool. The hair was gray or silver, bodies a bit bent, and many wore sunglasses.

An announcement was made—"no recording please". People just ignored this, as they do everywhere nowadays. I was at a Brian Wilson concert a couple of years back and I was amazed to see that every second person in our row had a smartphone out and was taking video of the show. I think that train has left the station, Van or Van's managers.

At the end of the show, you couldn't mistake the fact that it was over. He left the stage very quickly, the house lights came up, and despite the two thousand or so people on their feet, clapping rhythmically and chanting "More!", there were no encores.

The other musicians played on, finished the last instrumental and the last notes, and then left the stage. The last one to go was the keyboard player who stopped to grin at the audience, pull out his own smartphone camera, and take a photo of the crowd.

Our route on the way back to Los Angeles was Highway 74, definitely a back road giving a much different perspective on California than the freeways do. Palm trees and cacti line the road, and glorious mountains frame this scenic byway. It's definitely in the category of what you would term a "twisty road", with amazing views that are pretty much reserved for the passenger; the driver doesn't take his or her eyes off the road. The motorcycle riders I saw must have been having a blast. I didn't see any RVs on this road.

The Coachella Valley spread out around us, and it was just magnificent. Signs pointed out the Santa Rosa Mountains, the

San Jacinto Mountains, the San Bernardino National Forest, and the Pacific Crest Trail. This began to look like horse ranch country and it looked less like a moonscape, with more trees and fewer rocks. My ears were popping and we reached an altitude of 4,917 feet, just before Keen Camp Summit. We passed a sign for Living Free Animal Sanctuary, which takes in dogs and cats whose time is up at public animal shelters. Its postal address is Mountain Center, population 550, a tiny place with just a market and a gas station.

We passed Junction and McCall Park, for horse camping only. This was a *very* twisty, narrow road with cliffs enough to satisfy the most addicted adrenaline junkie. A big part of the fun was looking back at the extreme road we'd just covered.

I could feel that we were starting to descend and by Wilson Road we were down to two thousand feet of elevation. The number of buildings, vehicles and feet of concrete increased and by Grant Avenue we were looking at urban scenery once again. The road took us through miles of suburbs to I-5 and we were back to the Interstate.

A few thoughts on L.A. freeway driving—as in any big city, you're dealing with speed, the condition of the pavement, and the other drivers.

I've come across two philosophies. One is, stay in the right lane, go slower and avoid dueling with the constant challenge of the drivers who've chosen the fast lane, but have to deal with all the on-ramps and vehicles entering the freeway, many of them driven by people who don't seem to have any notion about adjusting their speed or merging with the flow. Second choice is to take up residence in the fast lane, but the speed and the aggression of the other drivers can be terrifying. Mostly, when I'm on those super freeways I just want to get where I'm going as soon as possible. I've never seen any study that proves which choice, slow lane or fast lane, gets you there soonest.

California is like nowhere else. Yes, I know I could probably say that about every one of the places I've been but California is one of those places that found a home somewhere in my brain long before I was aware that was happening. The songs, the movies, the books, the references. Then once I got there for the first, the second, the fifth, the tenth times there was no mental adjustment needed. I don't think I'm unique in that experience. Who doesn't know the melody and the lyrics of "California Dreamin'", from the Mamas and the Papas in the sixties (and many elevators and shopping malls, more recently)? Who has never seen Hill Valley, California, in the movie *Back to the Future,* or heard the story of Marty McFly and his time-traveling DeLorean?

Might be a bigger number than those who remember the plot and characters of the one of the earliest stories about time travel, from American novelist Mark Twain's fifth novel, set in this next state.

Chapter Five

CONNECTICUT

A Connecticut Yankee in King Arthur's Court, published in 1889, is the story of a nineteenth-century New England man who finds himself in 528 AD. Mark Twain set it in one of his adopted states: he was born and grew up in the South but later moved to New York and spent a lot of time in Connecticut. A museum established in what was his house in Hartford, from 1874 to 1891, is on my radar for a future road trip.

But the route off the Interstate on this one was all about the seashore. We left Providence, drove south to Narragansett, just across the water from Newport (think of an inverted wishbone—that's the Rhode Island shore with Providence at the top). Then we crossed over into Connecticut, heading for the town of Mystic.

This is almost a mystical place name, to me. I first heard of it in the early eighties when a movie (Julia Roberts's first movie) with the title *Mystic Pizza* was on at the cineplex. I thought it was a made-up name for a restaurant, created by someone with a whimsical turn of mind when it came to pizza and its properties. It turned out to be the name of a town on the Connecticut shore, just as depicted in the movie. The restaurant existed at the time the screenwriter lived near it and is still open today.

We stopped by Mystic Pizza, on Mystic's main street, and the pizza was definitely exceptional. So was the Greek salad. The interior décor was quite entertaining, too, with movie posters, concert posters, and photographs of movie and rock stars. My favorite was the pairing of framed photographs of Keith Richards at about age twenty-two and then at age fifty-something. (I'm just guessing about the ages, by the way; it could have been fifteen and thirty-something.) A large video screen had the *Mystic Pizza* movie playing nonstop and a gift shop downstairs had everything anyone might collect: mugs, fridge magnets, T-shirts, DVDs of the movie. No sign of any branded lobster pots, though. (Lobsters figure prominently in the movie.)

Mystic is an historic town with buildings clustered around and downhill from a church on a hill. Another appealing feature of the main street is a large independent bookstore with a nice layout and a good selection.

In front of a museum-style information board all about transportation, I saw a rack of bikes that looked like they were available for borrowing. This is a terrific idea that is in place in many towns and cities, and what a smart way to get more people to get around the downtown without bringing more vehicles in to compete for parking and to slow everything down. It wasn't on my plan for the day and the car was what we were using, but I could see the benefit of having the option of choosing to bike around.

The road out of Mystic took us north and away from the very crowded strip that is I-95. We used that freeway on a road trip last summer, to get from New York to northern Maine, when we didn't have much time to spare. It has to be some of the most densely populated asphalt anywhere. It is very nice countryside and I'm sure that for the people who live here, away from the transportation corridor, there are some beautiful pockets of trees, town, and turf to call home. But you really can't see it while you're motoring along at seventy mph on the Interstate. Up to this point, that drive in heavy traffic, heading toward Boston, was my only exposure to Connecticut and I have to say, I wasn't impressed. Now I was, much more so.

We took Highway 85 north from Mystic and saw some lovely rolling hills. A short deke across 82 to 11, and we were on our way toward Hartford, which on the map looked like one more big yellow mass of thick population and bumper-to-fender travel. But the swing through Hartford was surprisingly easy and the roads relatively clear. Mid-Saturday afternoon rather than rush-afternoon-Friday probably had something to do with that.

We decided to take a pass on Mark Twain's house this time, and also on the other attraction we'd considered visiting, Gillette Castle State Park. This has no relation to the holder of the current naming rights contract for the stadium where the New England Patriots play football. William Gillette was an actor who was famous for portraying Sherlock Holmes on stage. He chose to build his retirement home in Connecticut, and construction took place over five years, from 1914 to 1919. He lived there eighteen years while continuing to tweak this fanciful castle made primarily out of wood, featuring walls, windows, and stairways that gave it a strange appearance unlike any other. I'm tempted to compare it to a Salvador Dali painting or an Antonio Gaudí church but even those associations don't quite work. The state of Connecticut bought the castle in 1943, renamed it (it was originally called Seventh Sister after one of the hills in the region), and over the years, has developed it into a tourist attraction.

As we cruised along between Mystic and Greenfield, which is the gateway to crossing the border into Massachusetts, I was listening for the Connecticut song on my Rumble Strip USA Off the Interstate playlist. It had been a lot easier to find geographically branded songs for Alabama, Alaska, Arizona and California but Connecticut was a challenge. Never mind the challenge for the DJ, think about the songwriter or the

rapper. What rhymes with Connecticut? *"Coulda loved you but…",*
"Gotta get outa this rut…", "Yeah, but the door was shut…".

What I found was "Connecticut" by Bing Crosby and Judy Garland in the forties and "Kylie from Connecticut" by Ben Folds. I also went looking for something about Mystic. I could have used Van Morrison's "Into the Mystic", but I didn't think the intent quite matched.

It was my opinion that you'd have to search really hard to find a scenic drive in Connecticut. But I was wrong. Although it may not have as many on the list of top thirty All-American Roads, or even on the list of scenic byways, as some of the other states, it still has a lot to wake up the eyes, if you get off the freeway.

So does the featured road in the next state, one that is the darling of motorcycle riders around the country.

Chapter Six

FLORIDA

My first drive down Highway A1A on the Florida coast came in response to a cloudy day in Georgia. Just too dull, too gloomy . . . the right thing to do was to get up and get moving. When a walk through our Georgia neighborhood didn't feed the need, I was the lucky recipient of a suggestion that we drive to Florida and check out Key West.

Who would say no? We left Savannah at four in the afternoon and by 7:30 p.m. we were stopping in Daytona Beach.

Many (most?) of the people heading south toward the Florida Keys use I-95. You use a lot less time and, in some people's opinion, you don't miss much, since long stretches of Florida coast come with very little view of the water or beach. But A1A has a mystique and a glamor that I-95 just doesn't have, and since I hadn't taken the coastal highway before, and I'd seen quite a bit of I-95 already, I was more than ready to have the car leaning east, nearer the water, as we went south.

Florida is just crammed with interesting regions and roads to explore. Others I've done (and will have to write about some other time) include Highway 301, which runs north–south through the interior and almost seems like a trip back through time, to the way all of Florida must have looked before the theme park developments, the space race, and the retirement tourism boom. You can visit the farm where Florence Keenan Rawlins wrote *The Yearling* (and I did). Another is Highway 41 through The Everglades and a fourth is Route 98 on the Florida Panhandle, along the Gulf of Mexico.

But if you had to pick just one, I'd suggest this coastal Highway, A1A at the northern border of the state, then Highway 1, farther down the map. Get ready for lots of sunshine, billboards for oranges, alligator farms, and seafood restaurants, and places to visit that you've seen referenced in dozens of books and movies.

Just over the Florida-Georgia border, you come to a couple of unique barrier islands that are well worth a visit. Amelia Island is home to an annual Concours d'Elegance that draws car people from all over the world. The town on the island, Fernandina Beach, is that wonderful combination of funkiness and sophistication. If history is your interest, they have Fort Clinch State Park, featuring fortifications built by the Spanish in the early eighteenth century and later modified and adapted as an important strategic base during the Civil War. After some restoration during the 1930s, then service during World War II, the fort and surrounding area were opened to the public after the war ended. Visitors now can see military life enacted there by state park personnel.

Not much appeal for me so I gave it a pass to head for the beaches near Jacksonville. These give you the iconic Atlantic white sand beach and deep blue water views, with miles of as much fun in the sun as you can handle. A little farther south and you come to St. Augustine, the oldest continuously occupied, European-founded settlement in the continental U.S., established in 1565. Its governance passed back and forth, amidst much violence and bloodshed, between the Spanish, the British, and the Americans, with the last handover taking place in 1819. There was a lot of pirate activity mixed in there, too.

It's a beautiful city with architectural creations and details that will boggle your mind. Much of its style comes from hotels built at the end of the nineteenth century by railway magnate Henry Flagler, who envisioned St. Augustine as a winter getaway for wealthy northerners. Once the railroad was extended down to Miami, with its warmer temperatures and American Caribbean flair, St. Augustine became less the 'place to be', although it has never lost its appeal for tourists, thanks to the automobile, the building of the Interstates, and Walt Disney.

I was entranced with the beauty of the historic buildings and would love to have the opportunity to spend more time there. But I had a plan to get all the way down to Key West and back within a week, so it would have to be just a taste of St. Augustine this time.

The next highlight on this road was Daytona Beach, another legendary location for anyone familiar with racecars or Spring Break movies. It was cool just to drive past the track, even though there were no races on right then. Again, rain check.

Next morning we were on our way toward Key West. Google told me the drive would take six hours and forty-nine minutes. Why do I always look at the time it states, when I have asked for distance? The web page gives you both but somehow six hours and forty-nine minutes tells me more than four hundred nineteen miles. Actually, very rarely has the Google estimate of the driving time been completely accurate. It usually takes longer than Google suggests.

But let's assume it's somewhere between seven and eight hours. For me, that's a good day, maybe the best day. Longer than that in a vehicle and I get restless, tired from sitting for so long. Less, and I feel like I'm wasting time, taking too long to get there. Of course, you could take four days to do those four hundred miles. Actually, you could take ten or twenty if you had them. But the length of a trip and the timing is always a very individual (or couple-specific) choice.

And then there are all the choices about the way you take the seven hours apart. Go hard in the morning, have lunch, then putter along through the afternoon? Stay in the car for seven straight hours, drinking coffee from a travel mug, eating snacks from a bag or sandwiches from a to-go place, then arriving at your destination by mid-afternoon, with time to look around before dark?

You pick.

After Daytona Beach we decided to barrel on through. For this trip, Key West was the point, after all. Flashing past my window, I saw Titusville, then Cape Canaveral, then Cocoa Beach, then Palm Bay. A1A and Highway 1 seemed to dance with one another through a lot of these areas, but throughout the hundreds of miles I had the ocean over my left shoulder and the tip of the continent somewhere off through the windshield. Key West is called The End of the Road, and it's a compelling thought.

Vero Beach, Jupiter, Juno Beach, and then West Palm Beach crowd the coast of the peninsula like so many pearls on a string. At Palm Beach, Delray, Boca Raton and Deerfield, you are cruising past some of the priciest real estate in the U.S. The traffic is thickening, with lanes of highway seeming to appear out of nowhere to be added to the river heading south.

The area through Miami Beach and South Beach seemed to reach a maximum pitch of traffic, noise, and humanity. South Beach is a show, and even though I've seen a few things now, I was astonished by some of the sights there. The briefest bikinis in the world, no exaggeration. The most expensive, brightest colored cars. The most jewelry, the fanciest people. There might be richer people in other places, but they're probably the kind that drive sensible, older cars, have no mortgages, and hate to over-pay for anything.

The Art Deco hotels on Ocean Drive made me feel as if I were passing through an earlier time. I had to mentally edit out the modern people, though, and just focus on the architecture and the beach across the road. As the sun went down, more and fancier people came out to play. South Beach was certainly a scene, but I think I would be exhausted if I had to stay there long.

The next day we reached the other side of Miami Beach and somehow left the crowds behind as we glided along Highway 1 toward Key Largo and the Seven-Mile Bridge. People often recommend flying from Miami to Key West, but with each passing mile I was very happy that we'd decided on a road trip.

One of my all-time favorite movies (one of about a hundred) is *Key Largo*, with Humphrey Bogart and Lauren Bacall. A hurricane threatens the island and various gangsters attempt to commandeer the plot while Bacall stays cooler than a piña colada just out of a freezer-chilled blender. It's all very exciting and so very Florida. Taking a look at the real Key Largo was high on my list of wanna-do's, and apparently I wasn't the only one; a large billboard declared this the location of the famous movie. It was as beachy and as nautical as the movie might lead you to expect. We stopped for many photographs along the sand and a plateful of lunch at a dockside diner. Conch, lobster, and key lime pie are the local specialties on offer—not all on the same plate, of course.

Just to digress for a minute—if you haven't tasted key lime pie, you really must. The key lime is unlike any other lime, and if you don't have a piece of their pie while you're in the Florida Keys, well . . . you're just being rude, that's all. Would you go to Texas and not eat Tex-Mex? To Germany and not eat Black Forest cake? To Switzerland and not eat Swiss cheese? To Ukraine and not eat Chicken Kiev? To Spain and not eat Spanish rice or a Spanish omelet? To Greece and not eat Greek yogurt? To Italy and not eat . . . I'm exhausted.

Key Largo is the launching point for one of the most amazing drives in the world. Highway 1 has been built out, into the water, and despite the evidence of habitation all around, you see that you are about as close as you're ever going to get to boating all the way to your destination. We passed Islamorada, an absolutely enchanting place, and then Marathon, not yet shaken by the impact of Hurricane Matthew in 2016 and Hurricane Irma in 2017. The sun was shining and the air so warm that I almost decided to stop and look for work somewhere nearby, immediately.

The Seven Mile Bridge begins at Marathon—there are actually two bridges. The newer one is the one I was traveling on. The older one, used from 1909 to 1912, was part of the Flagler Railroad extravaganza, and was called the *Knights Key - Pigeon Key - Moser Channel - Pacet Channel Bridge*.

I think *Seven Mile Bridge* was a brain wave, don't you?

The old bridge is open only to pedestrians and cyclists. The new bridge opened to traffic in 1982 and, besides traffic, it conducts water to points west, in addition to communications, via fiber optic cables.

As I drove across, heading for The End of the Road, the wind in my face and the sight of the water seemingly all around were just exhilarating. This bridge has been used in quite a few movies and TV shows and it's easy to see why: it is drama on pylons. After Marathon, it was Big Pine Key and then I was rolling into Key West.

The city's architecture and public spaces display the sort of whimsy you would expect in such a distinctive place as this. The pier at the very end of the land mass is the location for a sunset celebration every single night and the scene is a visual feast of eccentricity. I was there three nights and could have happily stayed three hundred, but for a number of more practical considerations we had to head back. It was time to exchange the palm trees for the live oaks and Spanish moss—not a terrible trade, really.

Key West is famous, of course, as one of Ernest Hemingway's homes. Idaho and Cuba also celebrate his sojourns in their locales; the writers who travel and give future Tourism Departments good cause to reap the benefits of their association with their community are the focus of silent but frequent appreciation. I think F. Scott Fitzgerald is almost as prolific a tourism planter as Hemingway. Samuel Clemens, better known as Mark Twain, is another who got around quite a bit. Charles Dickens crossed the pond; so did Lafayette, although his purpose was, perhaps, a bit nobler, as he was spreading notions of liberty, fraternity and equality while Hemingway was just illuminating the glories of fishing and bullfighting. (Apologies to all fishing and bullfighting fans. Comedy is cruel.)

By contrast, Jane Austen never went anywhere and you have to go all the way to England to find anything dedicated to or preserved because she visited there. Louisa May Alcott is another; her home in Concord, Massachusetts is just what you'd expect, but I did wonder—was she never anxious to leave and see a few other places?

It's one of my failings (or great successes, not sure which) that I see a dozen good reasons to live in almost every place I visit. In Florida, it's the palm trees, the oranges, the turquoise water, the beaches, the gleaming skyscrapers in Miami, and the spooky hidden spaces of the Everglades. The climate in February, the pro sports games, the citrus fruit.

In this next state, I found a dozen and one, and so it became home, for a while.

Chapter Seven

GEORGIA

My introduction to Georgia came on a road trip when I walked into a highway roadside restaurant and heard an Aretha Franklin tune playing on a set of exceptional speakers. People were bopping to the beat as they waited for their sandwiches or Coke. Heaven, for a music fan.

It's a big state (aren't they all?) and I could choose any one of dozens or even hundreds of Georgia roads to feature. I came very close to picking something in the Atlanta area—it is one of the fastest-growing, most glamorous urban areas in the U.S., after all—but I decided to go for my own neighborhood and a road that runs through it—Highway 17 near the coast.

Coastal Georgia is really a very small part of the whole state. Unlike Florida, which is a lot of coastline and comparatively little inland, Georgia is shaped like a jug lying on its side, with the mouth to the east. The city of Savannah cozies up to the South Carolina border, and from there you can drive the Interstate to get to Jacksonville, Florida's most northern city, or you can take the coastline-hugging Highway 17, a scenic route that carries you along the fringes of the salt marshes and the barrier islands that make this part of the U.S. so distinctive.

Beginning at the South Carolina border, you cross the Savannah River into one of the prettiest cities in the U.S. Unlike many other towns and cities during the country's Civil War from 1860 to 1865, Savannah was not burned and as a result, many of the buildings, from as far back as the 1730s, still stand. Whether on foot, in a car, or sitting in a carriage behind a horse, a sight-seeing visit to Savannah makes you feel as though you've been transported back through time.

Visit in the fall or the spring, and you'll see the city at its best. The summer months demand some stamina. The temperature is often in the high eighties and low nineties, and you'll never see a place on the weather app that so often reads "85 degrees, feels like 95". I've been there through two- and three-week periods when the temperature didn't fall below 100. Of course, it's not lethal, and there are plenty of other extreme climates where you have to make adjustments. In Savannah, it's living indoors and with air-conditioning, just like in Alaska, it's indoors and with central heating.

The coast of Georgia is dotted with barrier islands, each one joined to the mainland by a bridge. Tybee Island is one of the closest and sandiest; it's often referred to as "Savannah's beach." If ocean water, a long pier, and a main drag with souvenir shops and sidewalk restaurants are what you're looking for, Tybee is it.

A little farther south, a string of these barrier islands gives the Atlantic lifestyle to residents and visitors. Saint Simon's Island, Jekyll Island, and Cumberland Island—each one has a distinctive personality and geography.

Jekyll Island was the setting of the Will Smith movie *The Legend of Bagger Vance*. Saint Simon's is the largest of the five barrier islands, referred to as The Golden Isles of Georgia. It's right across from the Marshes of Glynn, a name that somehow always makes me think of something vaguely Celtic or an Arthurian legend or a Frodo quest something.

"And then the young adventurer set off across the Marshes of Glynn . . . "

The marshes are a feature of Coastal Georgia that I was

not expecting, but now that I've been there quite a few times they've become part of my mental landscape of the state. Before driving in, I had expected more of the wide white sand Atlantic beaches I'd seen in Maryland, Virginia, and North Carolina. But if you look at a map you can see that the coastline changes quite a bit, in this stretch between the Carolinas and Florida, and the marshes are a result and a cause of that.

They turn color with the seasons, changing from bright green in the spring and summer, through gold in the fall, and into brown tones in the winter. Home to hundreds of wetland species of birds, amphibians, and reptiles, the marshes throb with life. On a windy day, the grasses sway in the breeze; at dawn and dusk, the shapes and colors are muted and fuzzy somehow, and as far as the eye can see, the marsh looks like an impressionist painting.

Highway 17 reminded me of a comb, with the highway as the back of it and the smaller roads leading to each of the islands as a set of teeth. Saint Simon's Island (sometimes spelled St. Simon's Island) is a popular vacation spot for people up and down the coast. It's just as warm in winter and as picturesque all year round as Myrtle Beach or Hilton Head but a lot less crowded. Cumberland Island, the last one in the chain before crossing the state line into Florida, is a national park that does not allow motorized vehicles. If you want to visit you have to make a reservation and go over on a ferry. You can rent bicycles over there (or take your own along), but you have to be heading back to the mainland by 4:00 p.m. It's a glorious, windswept landscape with wild ponies galloping over sand dunes and exotic wildlife offering incredible photographs in almost every direction you turn your head.

The seasons in Georgia are very distinct. This is not one of those places where the temperature stays about the same most of the year and the look of the sky seldom changes. Summer is hot and incredibly humid. Fall brings hurricane season (although officially, it runs from May to November, the peak months are September and October). The winter is frequently cloudy, and cooler than you might think, while the spring brings jasmine and other flowers, along with a dusting in some areas of what's called "yellow snow" or "Savannah snow" when the oak trees start another cycle.

The live oak trees are another thing I love about Georgia. There is nothing like an alleyway of them, draped in Spanish moss and bending toward the center, making a canopy, a tunnel of branches.

That first Sunday drive from Savannah along Highway 17 to the Florida line also introduced me to another distinctive facet of Georgia that is just as pronounced as the good music you hear everywhere. This is the Bible Belt, and I think you might find the churches are almost as numerous as those live oak trees. When we stopped for lunch at a dockside restaurant that featured delicious fresh seafood sandwiches, fresh-squeezed lemonade, and Georgia peach pie for dessert, I was surprised to see a large family at a round table to our right stop talking as soon as the servers showed up with their plates full of lunch. They joined hands and bowed heads. The oldest man said a blessing, they all said "amen", and then they tucked into their meal.

Later that day, when we stopped for gas and water, I saw another group standing beside the passenger door of an RV with Georgia plates. Again, hands clasped, chins sunk to chests, eyes closed, lips moved. I come from a part of the continent where praying is seen as a very private act, and yet really, why? Why not say some words and make a physical connection with those you love before sharing a meal or miles in a vehicle in traffic? People will let strangers see them eat, drink, sing, argue, fight, hug, and kiss in public . . . why not pray?

As we rode along on Highway 17 I saw a lot of travelers equipped for many different kinds of leisure activities. Bass boats for fishing, kayaks, jet skis and water skis—these are coastal communities, no question. I also saw quite a few vehicles (perhaps even the majority) displaying some sort of bumper sticker or decal declaring an allegiance to a pro basketball or football team. Actually, a lot of them referenced college teams (again, perhaps even the majority).

You can do many things in Georgia but one of the things you can't do is ski. You *can* drive a bit of a distance from Atlanta or Savannah, to North Carolina, Tennessee or Alabama. Or you could get on an airplane to Boise, as we did, and from there take a short drive off the Interstate to one of the country's oldest and most iconic resorts.

Chapter Eight

IDAHO

The line amounted to a grand total of three people. The Zig skied up to the door of the gondola, turned and waved a ski pole, and was on his way . . . and this was definitely 'off the Interstate'.

We drove into the Idaho countryside in order to get to one of the most iconic ski resorts in the United States: Sun Valley. This was the site of the first chairlift on the North American continent. Developed by the Union Pacific Railroad in 1936, Sun Valley was the playground of movie stars, national politicians, professional athletes, and other celebrities. It was the setting for the movies *Sun Valley Serenade* with Sonja Henie and *Ski Party* with Frankie Avalon, and the inspiration for a song that the Zig had set on replay, "It Happened in Sun Valley".

It has the largest automated snowmaking system in the world (which is quite amazing, if you think about Italy, France, and Switzerland, etc.). It is home to dozens of Olympians and, along with the city next door, Ketchum, has had quite a lot of appeal for celebrated writers, actors, and business people, as well as athletes, with Ernest Hemingway, Tom Hanks, and Bill Gates just a few of the bold-faced names that have bought property and spent time in the Sun Valley area.

Our day started in the city of Boise, which is an attractive urban place surrounded by incredibly clean air. They grow a lot of potatoes in Idaho and, being Irish, I like me some potatoes. My favorite meal in all my visits to Boise so far featured an appetizer of potato skins, a potato soup, and a baked potato for the main course. Somebody ought to invent a potato dessert. (What's that, you say? "Mashed Potato Truffles with Chocolate Chips"?)

Now, let's talk about the roads for a while. (Motorcyclists almost always look at the road first, not the destination; I like to contemplate both.) I-84 is the Interstate, connecting to Oregon in the west and Utah in the east. You've also got some I-86, I-15, I-90, and I-184, all in Idaho.

It takes just under three hours (depending on your speed, of course) to get to Sun Valley from Boise. We started out on I-84, with the sun lighting up the horizon. I loved the big sky and flat, open vistas. You can take US 20, and come at Sun Valley and Ketchum from the south. You could also take US 21 to Stanley, and then drop south on 75 to Ketchum. This second alternative gives you more mountain roads, with the twists, turns and thrills active drivers enjoy. It takes about five hours but the scenery is worth every minute.

But US 20 is the clearer choice if it's winter, as it was when we were there. You're less likely to encounter weather or road conditions. It's a two-lane highway (but there are plenty of places to pull over or pull out to pass).

We drove part of US 20 on the way to Sun Valley and US 21 on the way back. On the way in, we saw numerous small private jets coming in to land. I'm not sure I could pick which route I preferred—hey, maybe I'll have to go back a few hundred times before I can decide.

The road was quiet, quaint, and surrounded by fields full of solar energy panels. I saw a lot of signs, directing us toward the country of the Old Oregon Trail, an historic, East-to-West wagon trail route that covered more than two thousand miles. I spent a little time trying to imagine travel conditions and the many ways in which they were different for those early pioneers. Of course, they were heading west and we were going east of Boise—that's the obvious one. Trying to find places to ford the Snake River without drowning the stock (and themselves)—those early migrants took their lives in their hands every day.

The land was so flat that we could see the rainstorm that caught up with us coming from forty miles away. We passed dozens of farms and signs pointing the way to an exploration of fossil beds in the region (not on my agenda this time). Just after we reached Shoshone, we made a left turn, and could see the mountains.

Fifty-five miles to go. I was making notes of places and sights to see the next time I passed this road: lava fields; ice caves; Magic Dam historic site; the location of the Bannock War, an 1878 conflict between the U.S. military and the Shoshone-Bannock Native Americans.

As we started to approach Ketchum, the vehicles become a lot more impressive and the private jet traffic picked up. In the hills around the town, no doubt there are million dollar chalets but I didn't bother to go exploring looking for them, either in person or online. We didn't have a lot of time, and the Zig wanted to ski. Sun Valley is on that bucket list of white steep places to slide down, and the mountain was calling.

As we approached the city limits, my jaw was just hanging down at the sight of the glorious mountains looming above. It always looks to me like these gigantic piles of rock are protecting the buildings, roads, and people that bunch together on the hillsides below.

These mountains are just stupendous, even if you know mountains . . . if you are from the East, that is. Highest peaks in those states go forty-five hundred or so feet. In the West, you're looking at a mountain that is nine thousand feet plus. And the snow is sugar.

We rolled through town slowly, looking for a place to park. There was some sort of art festival on and the place was jammed with pedestrians and visitors driving interesting cars. A cruise past the original ski lodge was on the agenda; after that, we went looking for the center of today's skiing action.

Ketchum is where Ernest Hemingway spent his time when not in Florida or Cuba. He bought a home there in the 1950s and killed himself there. He's buried in the cemetery. Ketchum is adjacent to the resort city of Sun Valley and lies in the same geographic dip, below Bald Mountain. Music and entertainers-wise, Peter Cetera of the group Chicago lives in Ketchum, also Steve Miller and Tom Hanks, I'm told.

I didn't see any of them while I was there.

But I did see a lot of happy skiers on the hill. All ages—is there anybody more adorable than a three-year-old on short boards? (Or a three-year-old anywhere, really.)

We stood in a very short line for the Zig's lift ticket. Skiing was not on my activity list today, unfortunately; a pulled hamstring from too long ago was reminding me that I'd be better off with a mug of something hot, in front of the lodge fireplace. I haven't skied much in recent years anyway, and I doubt very much that I could have kept up with him.

The lodge was a treat—a large space with good food, beverages, and live music. After a while, I wandered back outside to watch the kiddies on the bunny hill some more.

I saw a few whose fearlessness and joy made them look as though they were destined to be racers, one day. Maybe I was looking at the someday winner of an Olympic Gold Medal in downhill skiing in . . . what, 2034?

Chapter Nine

INDIANA

In this state, we celebrate winners of another sort. In the fall of 2018, I flew into Indianapolis, Indiana, the racing capital of the world. Yes, I know, it's a road trip book, not a flying book, and there *was* a road that I explored by car, north and to the east of Indianapolis, but I couldn't resist an opening nod to the race car and the Indy 500.

I saw the track from the air, as the plane landed, and that was cool. My itinerary didn't include driving by it or touring it this time, so it was even more appreciated that the flight path in, on a clear day, let us have a long look at the Brickyard and the Pagoda. This drive, though, was geared more to the rural nature of Indiana. If you are looking for space, this is one good place to find it (with nods toward Wyoming, Vermont and Montana, of course). I had planned a trip on some of the two-lane highways north toward Muncie and then east to the state line at Richmond. We had to get to a meeting with a client in western Ohio and the best choice among the airline schedules led me to choose Indianapolis, then a rented car for a drive east.

But first, the Zig needed lunch.

We decided to go to Carmel, an attractive city about a half hour away from the Indianapolis airport, north on 31. This was the other Carmel, the less famous Carmel, (compared to Carmel-by-the-Sea in California). Actually, the U.S. has quite a few Carmels—fourteen in total, according to my research source. (And, no, that's not the Zig—although it could be.) Carmel in California may be taking a back seat to Carmel in Indiana soon, though, as magazines are starting to name Carmel, Indiana as one of the top three places to live in the U.S.

I don't know about living there (that probably has more to do with economics, the cost of living, and the quality of the jobs) but if I were looking for a great place to hang out on a Saturday after a long week at one of those jobs, I'd be happy to find the Carmel Art and Design District.

We were rolling along Main Street, having just passed under an arch that announced the District when I thought I spotted a man kissing a woman on the sidewalk. You don't see that much anymore, especially in these days of other people judging PDA all the time. I took another look, and it seemed as though he was wearing something unusual, too. It looked like a sailor's uniform, maybe circa 1940. It was a long kiss and neither one moved from what looked to me like a posture nobody could hold for very long. As we got closer I realized it was a statue, a replica of the famous photograph of a sailor kissing a woman in Times Square on VE Day at the end of World War II.

This was just the beginning of several blocks of statues on both sides of the street: a man playing violin outside a music store, a woman walking a dog, an artist doing a painting. The design of the storefronts and sidewalk cafés looked classic, although I think they are a mixture of old and new construction.

Our destination for lunch was an historic building that served as Carmel's library for many years. Built in 1914 as one of the gifts endowed by Andrew Carnegie for libraries all over the continent, the library later moved to new premises and the building became City Hall. In the late nineties, it was sold and became Woody's Library Restaurant. A lot of the old equipment and books are part of the décor and the food was excellent. Ten out of ten.

Next phase was a bit of Interstate time, then off on 36 east toward the Ohio border. At least, that was the plan, but the navigator (that would be me) got us off course, somewhere north of I-70.

Indiana is very flat, and I would have thought that, with such a distant horizon, extensive visibility, and a windshield-mounted GPS device, finding my way wouldn't have been very complicated.

I was wrong. We backtracked, made a few U-turns, and came across a few highway road construction detours.

But this turned out to be a bonus. "Not all those who wander are lost", as J.R.R. Tolkien wrote in a poem, and our wandering took us into many corners of this part of the state that we might not otherwise have seen. Tidy farmhouses, almost all painted white, and sky-high corn stalks lining the highway were the repeated motif of the pattern, with occasional farmers, dogs, and tractors adding breaks of color and motion.

Although I grew up on the prairie, I've spent most of my adult life living near a coast and I love the views of the water. But I often have moments, watching the fields roll by on a road trip through all this land in the middle, when I feel as though I am looking at a huge ocean of another sort—a vast inland sea of growing things.

It was a bumpy road, four-lane divided, leading toward Muncie. Somehow I eventually got us onto 32E, and the truck traffic became a lot lighter. Somehow a few miles on, we were on 35S and on the outskirts of Muncie. (I do think map-reading is a fine art, by the way, and a GPS is not a magic wand.)

The lots became much larger the farther we got from the city, and soon we were in farm country again. Many of the houses were decorated with stars, in various colors, most looking as though they were made of metal. They call them barn stars, and they've been part of the decorating style in the Midwest for decades.

I also saw a lot of people out on riding mowers, cutting all that grass.

We passed a sign pointing to Wilbur Wright's birthplace near Millville, Indiana where a museum has been set up in the house. His younger brother, Orville, was born after the family moved to Dayton, Ohio. This museum and one we saw later in Greenville, Ohio are just two of many examples of how much effort the Midwest has put into preserving its history.

I've never seen so much corn in one place! But then I've never been to Iowa near harvest season either, so . . .

Longtime residents or people born in Indiana are called Hoosiers but no one seems to know why. There are lots of theories, having to do with Indian words and terms for various kinds of jobs, but nobody claims to know for sure. They call Indiana the Hoosier State. If it were up to me, I'd have nicknamed it after the corn crop. Or maybe the green grass, to make a nice contrast with the nickname of the state coming up in the next chapter.

Chapter Ten

KENTUCKY

Since I was a kid, horse racing has been a part of my life. Not a big part—we didn't own horses or race them. But my dad started taking me to the track when I was twelve, and over the years I've probably gone to watch the ponies run a few hundred times, on a dozen different tracks.

Going even further back, I remember my Irish grandparents sitting by their radio many afternoons, listening as the races were run and called. They collected racing forms, newspapers, magazines about racing, and winning tickets that my grandfather occasionally bought when he made the trek, by city bus, to the track. They got to know the names of the jockeys and the horses each season; they could discuss the race results for hours.

I also remember my Russian/Ukrainian grandparents on their farm. The horses were long gone, but my parents, aunts, and uncles had stories of the days when the barn sheltered horses that pulled wagons to get the kids to school and plows to prepare the fields for planting. By the time I got there, all that was left was tack—heavy collars, rusted bridles, worn and frayed reins, a few thrown shoes—and the smells of old leather and straw helping a little girl to imagine real horses in the stalls.

These horses were quite a different size and shape than the ones I saw later at the racetrack, of course. That scene had a lot more spectacle to it, too. Brilliantly colored silks; long line-ups at the betting windows; the horses in the paddock; the bugle or trumpet playing the call to the post; the horses on the track, so strong and fleet, with their shining coats, black, roan, russet heads held so proud. They are incredible athletes, both the jockeys and the horses.

Probably the greatest display of strength and determination I ever saw from a horse was during a steeplechase on TV when he lost his footing after a jump, fell to the ground, rolled, and scrambled back to his feet. The jockey held on, sliding off the saddle and toward the back of the horse, but then regaining his seat, and so the rules allowed them to continue.

And they won.

Now that was exciting enough to see on TV, but can you imagine it in person? Going to a racecourse and being in the company of the thoroughbreds is exhilarating from the moment you walk in. I've always felt that about any racetrack, so you can imagine that my heart was pounding like *I'd* just finished a run when I walked through the entrance at Churchill Downs in Louisville, Kentucky.

The Kentucky Derby is one of the most famous races in the world. The best three-year-olds in horse racing go into the gate, and at the finish line, ten furlongs later, one of them is THE best . . . and is poised to become—perhaps—the next Triple Crown winner. The Kentucky Derby, the Preakness, then the Belmont Stakes. Three in five weeks.

This famous racetrack was the destination on my road trip off the Interstate in Kentucky. The highway was 922 and the city was Louisville, where Churchill Downs opened in 1875. It's named for the family who leased the land for the track in the late nineteenth century. It is Churchill "Downs" because of the tradition that began in Great Britain around 1500 when horse races were held on grassy fields. "Derby" came from an important race long ago when, as the result of a bet between Lord Derby and Lord Bunbury, the winner got naming rights. Might have been the Kentucky Bunbury.

My adventure to the Kentucky Derby began just before the first weekend in May when we drove from Savannah through South Carolina, across North Carolina to Asheville, and north through Tennessee on I-40. When we crossed into Kentucky, the first thing I noticed was that an election was underway; signs were everywhere. One that attracted my attention was for the position of Jailor (apparently, Kentucky is the only state in the U.S. that elects its jailors). Given that many elections are just a popularity contest, I have to wonder what a person has to do to become a popular Jailor. Throw a lot of movie nights and parties? Order the better brand of pizza? Leave the keys in the door?

The first few miles through Kentucky showed me a lot of woodsy scenery. Every home on the roadside seemed to have a porch and, no matter how small the porch, a collection of chairs for resting and socializing. Every few miles, I'd see a barn with an intricate quilt pattern painted on one wall, often above what appeared to be the barn door. I looked this up—apparently, there are about eight hundred of them in Kentucky and they are part of something called the Quilt Trail, which began in Ohio in 2001 and spread to Iowa, then Kentucky, and eventually on to forty-eight of the states and several Canadian provinces, totaling thousands of these barn quilts now. County quilting guilds, 4-H clubs, and other organizations often get together to work on one that becomes the pride of the local area.

As the landscape became less a forest and more about geology, I saw a lot of rock cliffs with the road cut through near Tateville. At Burnside a sign declared "Birthplace of the Boy Scouts Organization" and at Lancaster "A Small Town with Great Pride".

I was seeing lots of farms with cows but no horses yet, except on the license plates. I recalled from an earlier drive that northern Kentucky is where I saw the blue grass, the long white ranch fences, the pastures with beautiful thoroughbreds grazing, and the Kentucky Horse Park. Just off Highway 1973 (called Iron Works Pike) and near I-75, this park, dedicated to the relationship between human and horse, celebrated a forty-year anniversary this year. The events they run there cover everything from show jumping to dressage to international horse shows. The museums feature collections about American Saddlebred horses, Arabian horses, and hunter/jumpers. My favorites at the Park were the Hall of Champions and the opportunity to walk around the barns. Numerous famous horses are buried here and many are honored with statues, including the legendary Man o' War. This horse raced undefeated as a three-year-old just after World War I; was chosen by *The New York Times* as 1920's "Athlete of the Year", along with baseball player Babe Ruth; and had more than one and half million people visit him on the farm to which he was retired to stud. He sired more than sixty stakes winners, inspired paintings, books, movies, and museum exhibits. When he died in 1947, at age thirty, the horse was embalmed and buried in a casket lined with black-and-gold racing silks; his funeral was broadcast on NBC Radio.

On this trip we were staying in the city of Lexington, about a ninety-minute drive east of Louisville, along Highway 922 (also called Newtown Pike). We went back and forth a few times, after getting there and before setting out on the morning of Derby Day. Each time we drove along, I was intrigued by an old stone fence that ran alongside the highway and when I looked it up, found out it was one of many that lace the state, the style and methods imported by Scottish immigrants in the 1700s. We also passed a marker noting the location of Coldstream Farm, a famous horse farm that was the home of Aristides, the winner of the first Kentucky Derby in 1875. Coldstream Farm now belongs to the University of Kentucky.

It also was now clean-glass clear that I was in horse country, particularly thanks to the streets named after famous horses like Man o' War Boulevard and Bold Bidder Drive, and to the dozens of small trailers on the highway, carrying horses.

Saturday morning, May 5, 2018, we got started early. This was the 144th running of the Derby . . . and the wettest ever. By the end of the day in Louisville, I would see nearly three inches of rain, complete with a flash flood warning.

We got very wet. How can I even begin to describe it? I am used to wet, you know. I lived on the Canadian west coast for more than thirty years, and I've been every kind of wet there is. But nothing compared to this.

At the hotel they were offering mint juleps in the lobby at eight in the morning. My comment of "it's too early for me" didn't seem to go over well and the two young women in nineteenth-century dresses and fancy wide-brimmed hats kept on trying to get me to accept the customary shot of bourbon. As the day went on and I got colder and wetter, I was regretting my choice.

Now, Derby Day is all about the hats, which you know if you've ever watched the event on TV. I had a lot of fun getting ready for this. We visited a long-established hat store in downtown Savannah and bought a beautiful white straw hat with a wide brim and a dark blue ribbon band. I picked feathers, fabric flowers, and various flourishes, added them to it, and that morning in Louisville when I climbed out of the car in the Churchill Downs parking lot I was joining thousands of other women whose heads were also decorated.

The men were not bad, either. The Derby dress code is dressed up, for both genders. The liveliest costumes seemed to be worn by the people heading for the infield, while those in the boxes and the stands looked like they might be going to a wedding or a graduation ceremony. Many of the men were in southern-style seersucker suits and quite a few others had opted for brightly colored pants—pink, coral, aqua—under sports jackets and ties.

Even with the rain, the place was packed. I checked later, and the final attendance figure was more than 157,000—and that was the eighth largest on record. (The record was 170,513 in 2015). "Braved the Elements" was the phrase used in the local newspaper the next day, and I did feel brave. The parking lot had puddles that put the water up to my ankles. When we got to the entrance gates, I was told I couldn't bring in my umbrella and my choices were to take it back to the car or just hand it over. A first-timer's mistake, even to bring it, although I might have guessed, given my experience at another big venue, at the Florida stadium where I saw the Miami Dolphins play.

They *would* have let me bring in a poncho, but the list of prohibited items was lengthy. No coolers, cans or tents. No computers, camcorders (remember those?), tripods, large cameras, or selfie-sticks for the small ones. No grills—like I'd want to do any cooking at Churchill Downs, while wearing a huge sun hat and a fancy summer dress!
No alcohol, no thermoses, no backpacks, no luggage, including briefcases—like I'd let him work on some weekend paperwork, while I was cooking dinner at the Derby!

No.

Just in case this is useful information you need to know, I've included a few more details. The following items (some obvious and some inexplicable) are permitted:

Food items in clear plastic bags (limit two bags per person, maximum size 18" x 18". No trash bags)
Can you just picture someone coming in with a trash bag filled with their groceries, anyway?
Water and soft drinks. Plastic bottles only (sealed, clear and unopened)
Hah! None of your imported mint juleps, now
Baby/diaper bags. Only if accompanied by a child (subject to search)
Yeah, I wouldn't carry a diaper bag unless I had to, either
Small cameras. None equipped with detachable lenses or lenses of 6" or longer
We don't want you taking any long-distance pictures, using telephoto lenses, of people misbehaving on the infield
Binoculars
We'll allow these because we don't want you rioting once you see how far

your seats are from the finish line
Sunscreen. Non-glass containers only
Completely irrelevant on a day when it rains three inches
Cellular phones, smartphones and tablets
Because nobody would dare suggest anybody be parted from their phone nowadays
Seat cushions smaller than 15" x 15" that do not contain metal arms and/or backs, zippers, pockets or flaps
If you have a tush bigger than 15" by 15", too bad for you.
Strollers (ONLY if carrying a child)
But where does that leave those women whose dogs need to be pushed around in a stroller? Oh, see the item below. No animals allowed
Blankets and tarpaulins (Gates 1 and 3 ONLY)
Given the rain and the cold, if I'd known blankets and tarpaulins were allowed at any gate, I might have equipped myself!

These rules were very helpful. Not only did they tell me what *is* allowed, they went on to tell me what's *not* allowed. I liked the order of things, too. First they told you what you *can* bring, then what you can't. I'd say that's kindly—and optimistic. Glass half-full, before glass half-empty. The following items are banned:

Coolers (Styrofoam coolers, ice available at infield purchase points)
We get it, everyone should buy their drinks, at $12 per, from the venue vendors
Pop-up or patron tents. No poles or stakes of any kind
Now this one stopped me to think for a moment. Okay, if it's raining hard maybe some people would want to bring in an umbrella or even a tarp. But an entire tent? Do they have to tell people not to?
Laptop computers and camcorders
So, I guess they don't want people multitasking and trying to get a little work done during all the waiting around for the horses. A good way to prevent family discord.

Selfie Sticks
Whaaaat? Now this will be controversial, for some people. Highly praised by others
Luggage (includes briefcases)
No office work or planning to sleep over
Duffel bags
In case you have one big enough to hid a grill
Wagons
What do they mean, like the kind you pull a kid in? Who brings those to the racetrack?
Umbrellas
Come on now, couldn't we have an exception on days when there is a Flash Flood Warning for Louisville?
Drones and remote-controlled aircraft
Now this is amazing. Can you imagine ever having to prohibit something like this ten years ago? Who had a remote-controlled aircraft, except maybe Blofeld or Dr. Strangelove. Anyway, use yours to spy on your neighbors or check out the parking availability at the mall or whatever but leave it at home if you're going to the racetrack.
Animals (with the exception of service animals for guests with disabilities)
I'm sure a lot of the women could get outfits or carryalls for their dogs that would match their Kentucky Derby hats—maybe even dogs that would match—but it's not allowed. I'm pretty sure this rule has to do with scaring the horses
Any items deemed dangerous and/or inappropriate
And they close every last loophole, leaving us only to wonder who is the 'deem-er'? We know we are the 'deem-ees'.

Once I got through the long line to get in, waiting patiently while everyone's purses were measured and umbrellas confiscated, I was thrilled to actually walk into Churchill Downs. It resembles many other racetracks and courses but the atmosphere on that day was distinctive—the energy, the excitement, the familiarity after dozens of television viewings of the event. People were elbow to elbow, moving along the concourse and into the stands, looking for their seats.

The rain seemed to have lightened up somewhat and it was a relief to come out from the covered concourse into the open air of the stands. One of the other bewildering things about the prohibited items list was that it didn't include cigarettes and cigars, and many people were partaking in the indoor area. The air was smoky and it was a pleasure to get outdoors, even if it was a little damp.

The fastest two minutes in sport, they call it, but there was a lot more to do and see at Churchill Downs that day than just those two minutes. For one thing, the fashion parade was enough to keep me entertained for the hours until the Derby was actually to run, much later in the day. It felt a bit like I was surrounded by wedding guests or people at opening night for a very special play or concert series. Food and beverage sellers roamed around the aisles like other sports events but the most popular item was the mint julep. I had mine, and it was good, especially on a chilly, drizzly afternoon. But one was totally enough.

The fashions were intense! I saw gorgeous summer dresses and suits, pastel colors on the women and men. Stiletto shoes everywhere (sometimes carried by women wearing flip flops, either because they'd given in to the pain and given up or because they were heading for a walk through mud and didn't want to ruin the expensive shoes).

And the hats! Feathers, netting, flowers, wide brims, fascinators, it was all there.

The men were in bespoke tailored suits, zebra-striped sports jackets, seersucker suits, bow ties, pink or coral pants, and small-check dress shirts. Almost everyone was wearing a plastic poncho to protect their outfits from the rain. As the afternoon went along, it poured harder and harder; didn't somebody say it was going to get better in the late afternoon? Apparently not.

The infield was where all the really wild costumes were. Most people at most Kentucky Derbies, even those with seats, would take a walk over to the infield at some point to get an up-close look at the costumes, but quite a few seemed to be taking a pass on that tradition on this extremely rainy day.

Our seats were near the finish line at ground level. Even on TV, it's a great thrill to see these amazing animals come pounding around the last turn and into the homestretch. Feeling the pounding on the ground and hearing the crowd cheering?—heart-stopping and completely memorable.

Justify, a three-year-old that had not raced as a two-year-old and was much less experienced than most of his competition, dominated this year's Run for the Roses. He went on, that spring of 2018, to win the Triple Crown, the ultimate prize in thoroughbred racing. The second race is the Preakness, held at Pimlico Race Course in Baltimore two weeks later, and the third is the Belmont Stakes, held in Elmont, New York about three weeks after that. It's a rare feat and the owner, trainer, and rider of the Triple Crown Winner find their names in horse racing history books all over the world.

So, I did the hat, the wagering, the mint julep midday (before it was five o'clock anywhere!) I bought the T-shirt and the poster, got the program, watched the horses and jockeys in the paddock, then the walk out to the track. We stood at the rail at the finish line, and watched half a dozen other races run, while we waited for the Derby, scheduled for 6:45 p.m.

I even braved the lineup to the women's restroom for a necessary break. (I'm not sure what other alternative there was, in an eight-hour day.) It was *the* longest lineup to a restroom I've ever seen. Dozens and dozens of women, some of whom were close to having miscalculated their timing on this.

It was not my favorite part of the day, nor was walking through the smoky concourse to get there, but it was all made irrelevant by a celebrity sighting on my way back to my seat. It was not one of the pop stars, movie stars or athletes who attended the Derby; their seats were somewhere else, I guess, probably near restrooms with no line-ups. But I walked past famous trainer Bob Baffert, whose seat also was somewhere else, but who had to get to the paddock somehow, so there he was. Bob Baffert had trained five Kentucky Derby winners at the point that afternoon when I saw him. It would become six later in the day when his horse Justify won the race. Later in the season, Justify would become Bob Baffert's second Triple Crown Winner (the first was American Pharoah in 2015). He is one of the most successful trainers in the history of horse racing.

As the afternoon rolled on, we gave up on trying to get over to the paddock to watch the horses walk and then the jockeys saddle up. It was just too wet. My hat was limp, like so many others', and my feet were soaked through. So—

We left early, skipping three and a half hours of wet misery and the risk of hypothermia, not to mention the gigantic crush of people who would be trying to get out at 7:30 p.m. We walked out to the shuttle bus back to the parking lot through puddles up to my ankles and found a river running through the parking lot. Back at the hotel, we watched the race on TV with a bottle of wine and a pizza.

I debated over choosing songs to illustrate the Bluegrass State. The obvious one is the one sung by the crowd before every Derby, "My Old Kentucky Home". Another one very much associated with the Derby is "Run for the Roses" by Dan Fogelberg. But I ended up coming back again and again to an old Everly Brothers tune called "Bowling Green". For Kentucky, as for the state coming up next, I went for a song about a city rather than the state itself.

So, sue me.

Chapter Eleven

LOUISIANA

Down in Baton Rouge. Way down in Baton Rouge... I can't think of Louisiana without thinking of this haunting song and Amos Garrett's incredible voice. I also think of the bayou and the hot, hot weather, thanks to so many movies and television shows. The few times I've been there, it's been winter, spring, and fall, near to Christmas, so I haven't yet experienced that searing heat on the Gulf Coast. But it's been close enough to sultry that I get the idea.

In September of 2017, I visited Louisiana as we were on our way home after a mandatory evacuation from Savannah for Hurricane Irma. We had stayed in Memphis and then headed south through Mississippi on Highway 61, the Blues Highway that Bob Dylan sang about on *Highway 61 Revisited*.

This highway runs north/south just to the east of the Louisiana border. Picture Louisiana like a boot with the toe pointing west and the sole resting on the Gulf of Mexico. We crossed the state line just after Woodville, Mississippi and after a few miles we were back on the west bank of the Mississippi River. The Mississippi Delta runs from Memphis, right down to the lakes and bays south of New Orleans, and after a few days in the land of the Delta blues, I was eager to experience the jazz of the Big Easy.

Highway 61 through northern Louisiana passes through countryside where you'll see a lot of rocking chairs on a lot of front porches. It gets major-hot down here and unless you want to live your whole life running from air-conditioned car to air-conditioned room, without any fresh air, on many days the best plan is just to sit outside in a rocker, fan yourself, and not make too many ambitious plans.

When we rolled into Baton Rouge, we couldn't miss the French flavor provided by the city's history. It is the capital of Louisiana and the Old State Capital building (which looks like a medieval castle) is now a museum. In fact, the whole place seems to be big on museums: the USS *Kidd*, a retired WWII destroyer that is on the river, is on exhibit to the public; so is Magnolia Mound Plantation, with its French Creole house, and the Louisiana State University Rural Life Museum.

Baton Rouge is also home to Louisiana State University and as in so many other states, college football is a big deal. The LSU Tiger Stadium is one of the top sights to see here, and I'm told that if you go you can also stop in across the street at a fancy zoo where they keep the latest of the Mike the Tiger mascots.

If it's the bayou country and the swamp that fascinates you, you can visit the Bluebonnet Swamp Nature Center and see armadillos, owls, and alligators.

We were just passing through, on our way to a stop in New Orleans and then a turn east. We drove into NOLA with the top down on my red BMW, stereo playing Louis Armstrong and Allen Toussaint. You can comment on many things about New Orleans, but one of the most important is music.

One of my all-time favorite TV shows was an HBO series called *Treme*. (spelled without the accent on the second *e*, but pronounced with it). It's the name of one of the city's neighborhoods, christened in the eighteenth century after Claude Tremé who bought the land from the original settlers.

The TV show is the story of a group of New Orleans residents putting things back together in the aftermath of Hurricane Katrina in 2005.

The series was controversial, with some people loving it and others not. I liked many things about it, but the main draw for me was the way they used music. The characters were attending live shows, performing in bars, festivals, and on the street. Most of the numbers were allowed to go full-length, something you don't see very often in a TV show.

New Orleans is one of those rare cities where you can't mistake where you are. The architecture, the climate, the people—all unique. I've never been there at Mardi Gras time, but I've heard enough stories to want to put it on my bucket list. On previous trips I'd explored the Garden District and ridden the streetcar along streets near Tulane and Loyola Universities, seen the Audubon Nature Institute, and walked past stately mansions that could be imagined to be really spooky after dark. French surnames are everywhere.

On another previous trip from New Orleans, to visit a business client, we'd driven south to a small center called Houma. Highway 90 snakes along toward Raceland, where you can make a turn if you want to go to Lafayette, or continue on to 182 toward Houma, which is about as far south as you can go in this area. The bayou stretched out on almost all sides, interrupted from time to time by a small town. It was a memorable landscape, one more to add to the diversity that is Louisiana.

Another time, just before Christmas, we were working in Mandeville, Louisiana at an office at the end of a long drive back and forth from the hotel, across Lake Pontchartrain on the Causeway. It's the world's longest overwater bridge—quite an experience to travel twenty-four miles over water in a vehicle, on a road.

During my first visit to New Orleans I stayed in Warehouse District, explored Magazine Street, ate beignets at Café du Monde, and sang along to "You are My Sunshine", the state song, with the band that came around to the tables during brunch at Antoine's.

I loved the city and even thought of moving there.

It wasn't to be but I jumped at any chance to put it on a road trip itinerary. On this trip, we decided to stay in a hotel on Canal Street, got in late, and planned to leave early.

The Saint was an attractive hotel with interesting lighting and life-size photographs of New Orleans streets and gardens put up on the doors to the rooms. The room we were given had two beds with labeled bedspreads, one 'naughty' and one 'nice'.

Before making that sort of choice, especially after a long day on the road, we had to have some dinner.

"I'll be back in a few minutes for your orders," our server said as she passed the menus across the table in a nearby restaurant that was completely empty except for us. That should have been my first clue.

I looked it over and wasn't surprised that I had to spend a long time making up my mind. Shrimp, mussels, oysters—just not my thing. And yet, what else would you expect in New Orleans, or near any coast? I finally settled on the crab and corn cannelloni, after making the Zig wait so long he was just about ready to starve.

The server was there the second I set down my menu. What else would she do, when there were absolutely no other diners in here? "What'll it be?"

"I'd like a glass of white wine," I said. "Then the cannelloni dish."

Zig gave his order, and then we talked over the day while we waited for the drinks. In a very short while, the pasta arrived, along with a salad.

But no wine.

She was about to turn away when I got her attention back. "Excuse me, but what about the wine?"

"Oh, y'all can't have wine. We don't have a liquor license right now."

Say what?

"Is the pasta okay?" she asked. "It looks good."

And it did, but that was beside the point, at that point. "No drink? In New Orleans, are you kidding me?"

"No, sorry, can't serve alcohol."

"Do you think you could have told us that before bringing the food? Or maybe there should be a sign or a note in the menu or something?"

She shrugged and walked away.

So the cannelloni *was* good, but that's not the reason I remember that New Orleans restaurant on this trip. Unlike other restaurants, they didn't ask me to fill out any sort of survey form or go online and rate whatever, so I guess I'm doing it here.

I'm very annoyed with the constant requests for reviews, by the way, so I've decided to cope with that irritation and keep my stress level down by making each request into a Haiku game. Every review is in the form of a Haiku poem (and I think there will be a book, eventually). So this restaurant would be

Expectation wine
Denied in a party town
But the sun rises

The next morning I was up early, with a plan to get all the way back to Savannah in a day. The sunrise over Lake Pontchartrain *was* gorgeous and made up for the drink disappointment.

The driving day going back to Savannah was more than twelve hours, longer than usual because of the heavy traffic—thousands of vehicles still in motion, thanks to Hurricane Irma. It ranked right up there with one of our other longest road days, from Virginia to Maine, on our way to Canada in summer of 2017.

Chapter Twelve

MAINE

Virginia to Maine was twelve and a half hours, and that day we passed through five of the largest U.S. cities: Washington D.C.; Baltimore; Philadelphia; New York; and Boston, with a lengthy cruise through heavily populated southern Connecticut, which might as well have been one long city.

In August of 2017 we set out on a three-week trip across Canada, in celebration of the country's 150th birthday. To get into position, on the east coast of Newfoundland, we first had to drive north from Savannah, and this positioning road trip put me in Maine for the first time.

Maine is a state of forest and coastline, big stretches of undeveloped country, and beautiful small towns. It always feels a bit presumptuous to me to be describing places where I've only spent a few nights or even a few hours. But how long does it take? A week? A month? Live your whole life there? That seems extreme. I don't believe that only those people who live in a state can write anything illuminating about it; people who land at the airport and have only a one-hour layover often pick up quite a bit.

So you're getting my impressions based on one night in Maine. I'm not claiming it's the definitive picture, and if you don't think I got any of it right—well, then, write your own book.

The roads we drove were Highway 1, and then 9, from Portland, Maine to the Canada-U.S. border. As in so many of the states, the differences between the rural areas and the cities are quite extreme. We started out, crossing the state line from Massachusetts into New Hampshire. We reached Maine, crossing the gigantic bridge and passing the naval yard and outlet malls. A few dozen miles on, it felt as though I was farther into the forest, farther into a landscape where I could imagine the ancient days. We took Route 1 most of the way, with the occasional drifting off on a side road toward the north; mostly I wanted to hug the coast.

A familiar place name we passed was Kennebunkport, with echoes of the George Bush past. This was the summer home of the forty-first President. Apparently it's one of the wealthiest communities in Maine and is the summer getaway choice for many along the Eastern seaboard. The village center is only a mile from the Atlantic Ocean, and the whole area has retained a nautical atmosphere.

The views along this side road are just amazing. It know it's an overused word and I just am stretching for something better, but I can't find it. My jaw was hanging open during the entire Maine portion of the road trip. Rocky cliffs hunkered down over deep blue water, with lighthouses guarding coves and stately mansions dominating properties that might have had views all the way to Spain.

Then, right in the midst of this nature-loving, faraway-from-anywhere experience, we drove into Portland. This coastal city has roots (or should it be anchors?) far back in nautical history. The historic section of downtown, the harbor front, is a visual delight of weathered, clapboard buildings and views out to what was, on this day, a misty dove-colored horizon.

As I travel around, I like to collect signs. Unusual

language, word play, puns, clever or humorous thoughts. I saw one of my favorites so far on the street in front of a well-established pub in Portland. It was a sandwich board with a chalk message: Beer consultant on duty. A beer consultant? Well, why not?

Portland has a happy vibe—young, family-friendly, friendly-friendly (even if you aren't there with family). We met some people just standing in the Starbucks line.

"Venti Frappuccino for Frank," the barista announced, then put the cup down on the counter in front of the two men and one woman waiting just ahead of us. No one moved forward and we settled in to wait some more. It was a long line but no one seemed annoyed by the wait. I heard a few sociable comments along the lines of "Nice day" and "Do you live here in Portland?"

A few minutes later the barista reappeared. "Are you Frank?" she asked the blond man with the beard.

"I was once. It didn't end well," he said.

She lifted the cup toward the second man, who was laughing so hard all he could do was shake his head. The rest of us were laughing, too, and the Zig shook his head when she pointed the cup at him.

The woman with the baby stroller stepped forward. "I'll take it."

The barista did one more glance up and down the line. No sign of anyone claiming it. *Going once, going twice* . . .

Too bad for Frank. His drink was gone.

As we drove along Route 1, we noticed the traffic thickening up near the Brunswick and Freeport areas. People come to this region for the shopping and the retail factories nearby, particularly LL Bean, which has its roots (or seeds?) in this area.

The Maine hunting boot was invented here in 1911, I was told, by a hiker who had the brilliant mash-up idea for a leather boot upper, sewn to a rubber boot sole and foot. By 1912 it was a success.

We stayed overnight in Freeport, arriving late but finding

a very friendly desk clerk. That really does make so much of a difference to the traveler: hotels should pay big bonuses to the ones who are very good at their jobs.

We got on the road early the next morning, heading up the coastline toward Thomaston, Rockland, Camden, and Belfast, then north toward Bangor, which I'd wanted to see because of the "King of the Road" song. If we'd continued east, we would have seen Acadian National Park and Bar Harbor, two other famous places in Maine. Again, we saw incredibly beautiful coastline, and filed away plans for a return, slower trip.

From Bangor, we drove Route 9 E toward Canada, cruising on a two-lane, very woodsy, isolated sort of road. I think we passed three cars every ten miles or so . . . quite a different experience from the conditions in the Pilgrim State, coming up next.

Sweet home Alabama, where, according to Lynyrd Skynyrd, Muscle Shoals has got the Swampers, who'll "pick me up when I'm feeling blue"

Florence, Alabama and the birthplace of the Father of the Blues, W.C. Handy. Turns out, his father believed that musical instruments were tools of the devil. Apparently, ol' W.C. didn't pay much attention

Anchorage, Alaska, the starting point for the 1,000-mile Iditarod dogsled race. Unless you're the lead dog, the view never changes

The Seward Highway along Alaska's Turnagain Arm. In the short days and long nights of winter, the waterfall is transformed into an ice cascade

A total lunar eclipse over the Grand Canyon in Arizona. The stillness and majesty of the moment defy description

Route 66 in Arizona. It may have "wound from Chicago to LA," but some of those travelers obviously didn't last the "more than two thousand miles all the way"

Palm Springs, California. An oasis in the desert that's been a magnet for golfers and gamblers since the days of Sinatra and the Rat Pack

And not far from the luxuries of Palm Springs, Route 74 takes you up through the mountains where the brutal desert is in charge

The Union Baptist Church has been keeping an eye on the antics below along Mystic, Connecticut's Main Street since 1861

For slices of both heaven and Hollywood history, nothing beats Mystic Pizza

Live Oaks arching to form a canopy across the road can only mean the barrier islands of north coastal Florida

Savannah, Georgia: "As sweet and clear as moonlight through the pines"

Skidaway Island, Georgia. Hurry? Who's in a hurry to go anywhere or do anything in particular?

On the way to Sun Valley, Idaho, winter playground of the rich and famous since the 1930s

Gentlemen, start your engines! The cars have been racing around the track at Indianapolis since 1911

Flat, flat, flat. Corn, corn, corn. Or at least Indiana can seem like that for mile after mile

Watching the incredible equestrian athletes run for the roses at legendary Churchill Downs in Louisville, Kentucky was a lifelong dream come true

The Kentucky Horse Park at the locus of thoroughbred country outside Lexington, KY. The statues seem almost as alive as the horses

Departing New Orleans in the early, early morning with the open highway beckoning us on to the next horizon

Portland, Maine was born of the sea and many of its waterfront buildings still keep their feet wet

Those who choose to march to a different drummer can find their inspiration in a walk around Walden Pond near Thoreau's Concord, Massachusetts

Henry David Thoreau spent two years, two months and two days living in one tiny cabin, with one room and one chair

Highway 61 at The Crossroads near Clarksdale, Mississippi, where bluesman Robert Johnson is said to have traded his soul to the devil in exchange for success

The grace of antebellum elegance in Natchez, Mississippi covers a terribly troubled past

Modern-day adventurers who want to hike in the mountains near Lincoln, New Hampshire, have some inspiring predecessors who set the bar really high

The oldest dance floor in the oldest restaurant in the oldest state capital in the country. Flamenco has been swirling here since 1835

Horse racing has been an integral part of Saratoga Springs, NY since 1847. The iconic Saratoga Springs Race Course opened in 1863

In Saratoga Springs, NY, even the street art is all about horses

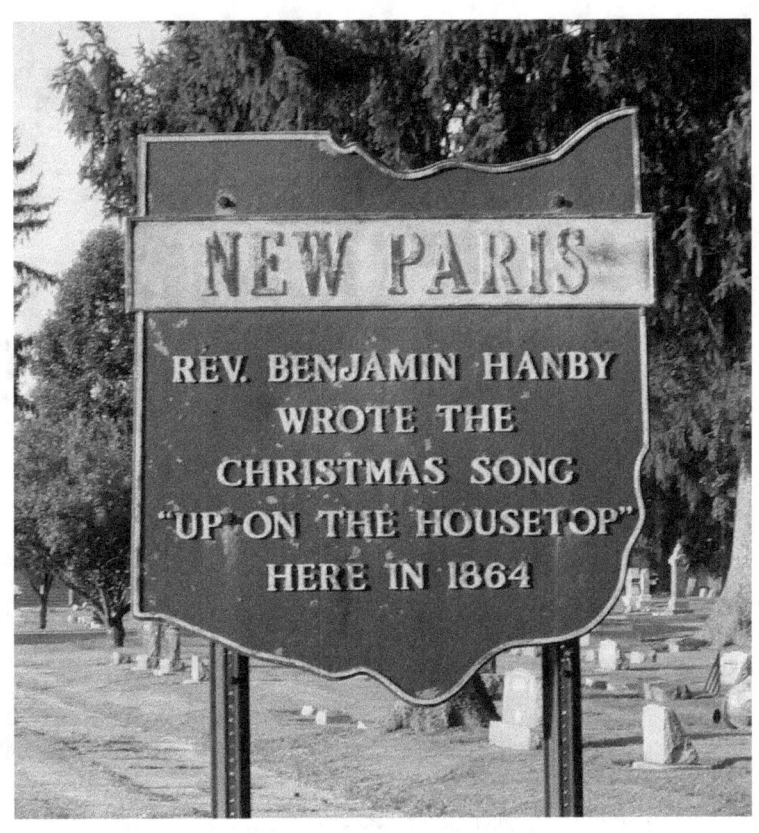

New Paris, Ohio. Since George Washington didn't sleep here, we'll work with what we've got!

Born in 1860, Annie Oakley became the darling of Greenville, Ohio. But her mother may not have first imagined her petite daughter hanging off the side of a horse while firing her six-shooter

The houses and the lifeguard chairs along Rhode Island's shore at Narragansett seem to stare out to sea, waiting and watching…

The Narragansett Towers are the only remaining part of the original Narragansett Pier Casino, built in 1883 and once the be-seen place for Rhode Island's social elite

The Battery in Charleston, South Carolina where the Cooper and Ashley Rivers meet and, allegedly, the citizens stood to watch the bombardment of Sumter Island and the outbreak of the Civil War

The stately antebellum mansions of Charleston keep the brilliant sun outside and preserve the cool dark shade within

In the heart of Memphis, Beale Street is the legendary home of the blues and the street where W.C. Handy, Louis Armstrong, Muddy Waters, and B. B. King, among many others, came to 'lay down some licks'

The sad side of Memphis includes the Lorraine Motel, where Martin Luther King, Jr. was assassinated on April 4, 1968

Austin, Texas, where they work hard to keep it weird . . .
And wonderful

"Don't drink and float." Some great advice when floating high above the Green Mountains at the annual balloon festival in Stowe, Vermont

It doesn't get more quintessentially New England than this view of the community church in Stowe. I've seen a lineup of photographers waiting to get this shot

Thomas Jefferson built a house, then went on to help build a country. He began working on his beloved Monticello outside Charlottesville, Virginia at the age of 26

The winding ribbon of roadway through the North Cascade Mountains in Washington made it feel as if the car were dancing

How many mountain winters has this lone pine in Sun Canyon, Washington seen? What stories could it tell?

Chapter Thirteen

MASSACHUSETTS

I always thought it was one of the weirder pop music milestones that a band from Australia, the Bee Gees, had a huge hit in the seventies with a song about Massachusetts. *Something's telling me I must go home*... Which just proves, I think, that artists can do whatever their creativity moves them to do, and logic need not enter the decision.

I discovered as I wrote this chapter that this song is one of the (thousands of) earworm songs I have in my memory.

I also discovered that Massachusetts is tough to spell correctly. You can either decide to copy and paste, or take note and memorize—more 't's than I thought and not as many 's's.

My excursion off the Interstate in Massachusetts started in Boston, which is, of course, on a couple of major highways, but is off quite a few too, so it qualifies, and I always enjoy getting to Boston. This trip was in mid-October and the leaves were turning to glorious shades of orange, gold, and red. Down on the Charles River, rowers were practicing, and the weather was perfect for scarves and even gloves. It was chilly, yes, but not as cold as my previous visit, when I'd happened to be there at the time of the annual Santa Claus Run and hundreds of half-naked fundraisers ran along Newberry Street, their skin as red as the Christmas hats they were wearing.

Boston does Christmas very well. The Pops Orchestra packs them in at Symphony Hall every year, and the festive spirit shows up in elegant seasonal décor up and down Beacon Hill.

It also does sports very well. Hockey, baseball, football. And advanced education. Across the river in Cambridge, students study at Harvard, one of the top universities in the country. It does fireworks well, too, with the Fourth of July event on the Charles River perennially popular. It does art, literature, architecture, history—and too many other activities and endeavors to list.

Except for one. I can't omit to mention that Boston does food well. Clam chowder. Cream pie. Lobster roll. Pizza. Fried clams (with fries and onion rings). Cannoli. Baked beans. On this visit, we stopped for an exceptional Italian meal at Copley Square.

Fortified, off we went on Highway 2 toward Concord. A very famous town, in literature and philosophy world.

One of the activities I enjoy from time to time on the road is searching out birthplaces of or museums dedicated to writers who have made an enduring mark. Concord, Massachusetts was home to one of the first authors I loved, as a young reader—Louisa May Alcott. Is there a vintage woman alive who doesn't know *Little Women*, or remember Meg, Jo, Beth or Amy?

The house where she wrote her novels in the mid-nineteenth century has been made into a museum. We found our way to it after a tour of the town. This was a couple of weeks from Halloween, and most of the porches and doorsteps were adorned with plump pumpkins. Quite a few had broomsticks.

Parts of Louisa May Alcott's Orchard House were only open for guided tours. The Alcotts moved there in 1858, when her father bought two houses (circa early eighteenth century) and put them together. The areas that I saw seemed quite fragile—old wood, delicate furniture, and aging construction. It seemed completely understandable that they would try to control the traffic.

As in so many of these historic preserved homes and buildings, I'm struck once again with how small the people must have been and how cramped their indoor environments were. I saw low ceilings, sloping floors, narrow hallways and steeply pitched stairs.

I also always notice how close to nature they were and how they'd react if they were dropped down into a twentieth-century, fully paved city. Concord, Massachusetts, even today, has a lot of open space, and Louisa May Alcott had a huge area to roam around with numerous serene, beautiful vistas.

Another Concord resident, Henry David Thoreau, went looking for even more nature, walking off from his family home in town, toward Walden Pond, where he lived in a tiny cabin, meditated, and wrote philosophy.

After seeing Orchard House, we made our way about a mile and a half to Walden Pond. When I was in my twenties, quotations from Thoreau turned up on posters everywhere and the imagery of *marching to a distant drummer* or the *mass of men with lives of quiet desperation* or *living the life you have imagined* became entrenched in the psyches of several generations. I was eager to see the place where these thoughts dove into the pen of this writer.

The pond itself is beautiful and I could easily understand how he felt so inspired. We walked on its beach (and I was amazed at the hardiness of several families who were in, swimming). Then we walked over to the cabin itself. He lived there two years, not just the one that he documented in his book. The site was discovered in 1945 by an archaeologist, nearly one hundred years after Thoreau left Walden Pond. The actual cabin was taken down shortly after his time there but images taken at the time remained, and a replica stands at the site now. They also found artifacts from his stay that have been preserved at the Thoreau Institute.

I did get a bit of a vibe of the time, the solitude, and the one of the key legends in the land of the Delta Blues, memorialized in song, literature, and film. Here you will also find the Delta Blues Museum, the Rock and Blues Museum, and other collections of material seminal to the development of one of America's defining contributions to world culture.

It was a flat, two-lane, mostly straight highway, lined by small towns and cotton fields—quite a change from the Interstate, with countless versions of the same chain stores, gas stations, and fast-food restaurants.

One of the first things I noticed was that there were so many churches along the way, many with unusual names like the "Get Recovered Ministry". The Mississippi River was to my right as we cruised south through the state. I've flown over this area a number of times, and the view of the Mississippi Delta from the air is absolutely amazing. The boundary with Arkansas runs, pretty much, right down the middle of the river.

Riding along and looking across the water toward Arkansas reminded me again what a fascinating study the history of border-making is. Who picked the river as the dividing line and why?

I'm sure there is a book about it somewhere.

I took note of the churches, the cotton fields and quite a few casinos. I guess in this state, as in so many, casinos have turned out to be a new type of gas for the economic engine.

The rain was pouring down, bouncing from the pavement. The hurricane-linked weather had reached a long way inland, and we were seeing some of the effects.

We passed a sign for the Mississippi Mounds. The Mound Builders were Native Americans who, over a period of four to five thousand years, built earthen structures to serve as locations for ritual and burial ceremonies. Sometimes they were the location of the chief's home. They are located in various spots all over the continent and in many areas, such as this one in Mississippi, have been studied and preserved as part of the National Historic Register.

It would have been interesting to see and explore them but the rain was just too intimidating. Next time.

intensity of contemplation that took place there. It wasn't as remote as I expected, although I realize I was experiencing it as a twenty-first-century woman who'd arrived there by car on a paved highway, traveling sixty mph. Imagining it as a man, walking, and the distance seemed much greater, and the transition from town life, in Concord, much greater.

It was a tiny cabin, and I could well visualize Thoreau absorbed in his books and his writing, as a way to live beyond the restrictions of his reality. As with Orchard House and other historic places of that sort, I took note of how very small everything was. People just didn't take up as much space as they do nowadays.

Maybe if we had less space, we would be more contemplative, too.

As we drove through Salem I could see a lot of witchy connections, all humorous. People were in costume too, getting their Halloween thing on early, particularly in the neighborhood of the Salem Witch Museum. We took US 1 to get back to Boston, a nice road much more appropriate to the long ago times I'd been thinking about all day than the nearby Interstates would have been. Not a highway I'd ever heard of, though—unlike the one coming up in the next chapter.

We stopped for an ice cream in Corinth, where the clerk said, in an accent I barely understood, "Have a blessed day." This is Bible Belt country, and God and Christianity are a daily part of life.

It's also contradiction country, and sorting it all out is beyond my powers of observation or vision. I'm going to stick to something I know and something within my abilities to comprehend.

Music.

As we cruised along the highway, I was listening to the Stax 50th Anniversary Collection—Booker T and the M.G.'s, Otis Redding, Sam & Dave, Carla Thomas, Isaac Hayes, Wilson Pickett, The Staple Singers. These artists from the sixties and seventies have always been some of my favorites and I was just thrilled to be in a part of the country that was so essential to them.

Of course, the sixties and seventies aren't the be-all and the end-all, as they might say around here. Music history runs rich and deep, with a series of markers along the Mississippi Blues Trail on Highway 61 recounting the lives of the men, women, places, and events that shaped the story, all the way back to the nineteenth century.

We were headed toward Tunica, and there were very few other cars. I was watching for the Blues Trail Markers, some of them, anyway. I had no hope of seeing all 198, the total at the time. They're still adding more.

The first one I spotted was the Highway 61 Blues marker, which tells of the history of the music and of the road, and of the way the theme of travel runs through the music. Dozens of blues artists have written and recorded songs about Old Highway 61, including Sunnyland Slim and Big Joe Williams. Many were born or lived near it, including B.B. King, Howlin' Wolf, Muddy Waters, Robert Johnson, Honeyboy Edwards, Sam Cooke, and Jimmy Reed. It was the road many traveled north, seeking fame and fortune, and in its first form, in 1900, it was a gravel road that began in New Orleans, went through Baton Rouge, into Mississippi, to Memphis, through St. Louis and St. Paul, Minnesota (Bob Dylan's home state) and to the Canadian border.

The markers are rectangular, colored a vivid blue, and very text-heavy. I couldn't read them, as I zipped by at full speed, and so I planned a few stops at important ones along the way. The water was still coming down from the sky like a Hawaiian waterfall and I didn't want to get soaked, or spend more time than I planned in Mississippi, so we weren't stopping at every one.

The one that was a 'don't miss' for me on this very quick trip through the state was at the crossroads. I've seen photos of this spot, where blues legend Robert Johnson is alleged to have sold his soul to the devil in return for guitar genius. The scene is always lonely and windswept. With the miserable weather on the day I passed through, the feeling was even more desolate than had come through in any of the photographs. I took a few of my own but they didn't turn out.

And it was weird, but my phone wouldn't work properly there.

We had so much ground to cover and the weather was so horrible that I didn't want to linger. A careful, relaxed exploration of the Delta Blues Museum and the Rock & Blues Museum in Clarksdale would have to wait for a future visit.

Highway 82 crosses 61 at Leland, leading east to Indianola, B.B. King's birthplace. His connection with Tennessee and Memphis is well known, and in addition to all of the other places, his name lives on high over Beale Street on a restaurant and music venue.

Highway 82 also goes east to Cleveland, home of the Delta State University mascot, the Fighting Okra. That's the unofficial mascot, I was told. The *official* one is the Statesman (and the female athletes are called "the Lady Statesmen", no kidding). In the late eighties, according to Wikipedia, students began to joke about the lack of athletic competitive fuel built into the image of a "Statesman". Someone suggested that even a vegetable as a mascot would have more power, and support for an unofficial mascot, the Fighting Okra, began to grow. It was eventually formalized in a student vote.

I love the idea of an aggressive vegetable. Mean and green. So did many others in Mississippi, apparently, because the idea took off and has drawn national attention. Delta State U is one of eight publicly funded universities in Mississippi and one of thousands in the country, but how many have a mascot like this?

We stopped in Cleveland for gas and saw two sheriffs' trucks (big ones with windows fully dark) and a state trooper car, all within four blocks.

No athletic or belligerent vegetables, though.

Long, flat stretches of highway made up most of the view through this stretch, occasionally interrupted with small towns and villages. Then we reached the Natchez Trace Parkway. No trucks are allowed on this National Parkway It crosses three states and attracts bicyclists, campers, hikers, history buffs, and road trippers from across the continent to a route that was used all the way back to the prehistoric animal days. If we were to take it north, we'd eventually arrive in Tupelo, which is a significant site on the Mississippi Blues Trail because it's Elvis Presley's birthplace (and significant on my turntable because it's part of the title of one of Van Morrison's best songs).

But it was not on my itinerary this time. We were heading south on 61 toward Vicksburg, the birthplace of Willie Dixon, one of the most influential blues musicians. He was one of the ones who took the music to Europe in the sixties. Covers of his songs, recorded by the Rolling Stones, Led Zeppelin, and others, spread the sound to new ears.

Vicksburg is also the location of a significant Civil War event in 1863, a forty-seven-day siege which led to the city's surrender the day before southern general Robert E. Lee was defeated at Gettysburg, both considered turning points in the war.

We were heading for the Louisiana border now, intending to spend the night in New Orleans. Some of the songs written about Highway 61 refer to it ending at the Gulf of Mexico but that's a bit of geographic license. Old Highway 61 actually ends at New Orleans (although the Blues Trail itself includes Gulf locations and some important out-of-state locations, too—Chicago and Los Angeles, for example).

Louisiana is known as the Bayou State, Mississippi as the Magnolia State. The state highlighted in the next chapter has the nickname The Granite State—but it's better known for the slogan shown on its license plates.

Chapter Fifteen

NEW HAMPSHIRE

*L*ive free or die. That's what it says on the state license plate and, of course, I had to look it up. It's an official motto, adopted in 1945, and Wikipedia says it comes from a speech given by New Hampshire's most famous Revolutionary War soldier, General John Stark, in 1809. It was already a popular slogan of the French Revolution and it had been said in other places and other ways, as well—in the American Revolution ("give me liberty or give me death"); in Brazil ("Independence or Death"); and in Scotland ("freedom . . . which no honest man gives up but with life itself"), for example.

New Hampshire's motto is probably one of the most memorable, because it's short, to the point, and unencumbered by old-fashioned words (not to mention, being available to both genders). Even though I've seen it thousands of times now, it does catch my attention every time, after reading a few million words like "Scenic" or "Colorful" or "The First" or "Vacationland".

Another one I used to notice back in the day was "Seat

Belts Fastened?" which was on the Ohio plates. I like their concern for my safety and it's certainly just as commanding as the New Hampshire plate, since we all know a rhetorical question when we see one. You might say it's a bit less political but maybe not. Certainly it's in opposition to the New Hampshire message; a lot of people would say there's not much freedom behind a seat belt and even less if it wasn't your choice to wear one.

New Hampshire, by the way, has no mandatory helmet law, which makes some motorcycle riders very happy. Seat belt laws? Yes, but only if the passenger or driver is under eighteen years of age.

Besides the seat belt question, Ohio has also used the slogan "Birthplace of Aviation" because the Wright Brothers' hometown was Dayton, and because Congress said they could (in 2003). Also, historians have concluded that Orville and Wilbur did their design work and built the first airplanes in their shop in Dayton, Ohio.

North Carolina had also claimed to be the Birthplace of Aviation, because the Wright Brothers' did their early test flights at Kitty Hawk on the Outer Banks. Now it has "First in Flight" on some of its license plates, along with "First in Freedom", which New Hampshire might contest, unless a few too many of them had to take the "or die" option and now they're outnumbered.

Our road trip off the Interstate in New Hampshire took in part of the White Mountains in the northern part of the state. New Hampshire has Massachusetts to its south, Maine to its east, Canada to its north and Vermont to its west. We started near St. Johnsbury on I-93 and the Zig was in his glory, eating up the twisty road in the BMW 3-series. Actually, the traffic was so light in this part of the state that you really didn't have to look for a side road. I'm told it's a whole different picture in fall foliage season and in ski season, especially after some new powder, but on this day in early September we had almost the whole highway to ourselves.

We were heading south and as we got closer to the ski

resorts, the volume of traffic picked up. Cannon Mountain loomed up on the right, and you could see the outlines of the ski runs even without their winter coating of white. New Hampshire is forest, of course, and the beauty of the trails and canopies have turned this area into a destination even when there is no snow.

Franconia Notch is a famous spot on I-93 and in the fall months, before stick season, when the leaves are all still on the trees, throbbing with colors from red to gold to yellow, the views through the Notch are just spectacular. "Stick season" got its name because the leaves have all fallen from the trees and the branches look like sticks—I guess they actually *are* sticks, or would be, if someone broke them from the tree.

The side road I'd picked was Highway 112, also known as Kancamagus Highway. It starts on I-93 and cuts through the White Mountains to Conway (or vice versa, of course). The ski town of Lincoln is at the crossroads. I could tell from the road signs that even though it was a bit sleepy today, in leaf peeper season or winter sports season, this little town would be bursting with tourists. The signs read "No Parking next 1/4 mile" and there was a sign posted every few hundred feet.

The traffic thickened up and we drove into town behind a herd of motorcycles. It was just the sort of road that riders love. One of the highlights of the morning for me was approaching a hairpin curve (labeled as that, with a 25 mph suggestion) and following a bike around it. We drove on, into White Mountain National Forest, but a short distance down the road, I saw him pull over to the right, and then, in the side mirror, saw him cut across traffic to head back in the reverse direction. About an hour later, when we'd gone as far as I wanted to along Highway 112 and were heading back toward the Interstate, I saw him again, near the same hairpin curve, going past us in the other direction. Had he been going back and forth on that same turn for more than an hour?

We stopped at Hancock Notch for an amazing view of the mountain range. The (very helpful) information display told us about the passion that people had to climb these mountains even back in the nineteenth century, and how conservation had become so vital as the decades went past. But even with the understanding of the impact of human traffic on the mountains, there still was (and is) a drive to climb and conquer them, with "peak bagging" a perennial hobby in New Hampshire. There are forty-eight peaks over 4,000 feet and those are the ones you want to bag, and brag about.

Kancamagus Scenic Byway is about thirty-four and a half miles long, running beside the Saco River. I'd love to come back, see it on a bike and stop much more frequently, maybe hike some of the trails, maybe bag a mountain peak. But that would make it a different sort of trip, not a road trip, wouldn't it?

That would take a lot more time, too, more than the half day I planned as we made our way toward Massachusetts and Rhode Island. New Hampshire was quite an unknown to me before this trip, unlike the state coming up in the next chapter. I had never followed any New Hampshire teams, never read any books, heard any songs or watched any movies about New Hampshire. A secret gem, in a way—while the next state was one big chunk of turquoise in the
middle of an outsized belt buckle.

Chapter Sixteen

NEW MEXICO

New Mexico is one of those states that has, for me, a glitter of glamor. Maybe it's the echoes of songs I heard a thousand times and memorized during my childhood. (Why does that happen? Why, when I have trouble remembering where I was a week ago Tuesday, can I remember every word of every line of a Buckinghams song from 1970-whatever?)

Maybe it's the movie scenes of the great open spaces of New Mexico, the pueblos, the architecture, or the food. Maybe it's Georgia O'Keeffe. Whatever it is, the drive through New Mexico was one I looked forward to. It delivered on the expectations in every way.

New Mexico has Arizona to the west and Texas to the east—it is as 'western' as it can get. On this road trip we drove mostly on Interstate 25, wandering off onto some of the smaller highways occasionally. Unlike in the more populated states, a lot of the choices didn't really appeal to me, given the time I had available and the destinations I wanted to see. There were too many of those and I had to drop a few off the list (and put them on the 'next time' list: Silver City, Roswell,

Carlsbad, Santa Rosa, and Taos).

This trip began in Las Cruces in the southern part of the state just across the border from Texas and carried on to Albuquerque and then to Santa Fe. (I have almost as much trouble spelling Albuquerque as I do Massachusetts.) From Albuquerque to Santa Fe, you can also drive The Turquoise Trail, a Scenic Byway with the more ordinary name of State Road 14, running about fifty-four miles just slightly to the west of I-25.

The scenery in the high desert was stunning and the weather was perfect. This was a trip taken in the fall and the summer heat had broken. The sky was incredibly blue and the air unbelievably clean.

In Albuquerque, the buildings and the architecture took over. I don't know what it was but there was something about this city that made me feel instantly relaxed. We walked the Old Town area for hours, exploring adobe houses that had been there for centuries and eating New Mexican food. I saw a glorious nineteenth-century structure that houses San Felipe de Neri Church. The smaller buildings hold hundreds of small shops, all privately owned and individually sourced. No chain-store, bulk purchases there! The hours were a bit unpredictable, though, since each shop keeper sets his own.

I enjoy historic places where it seems easy to imagine the people of two or three hundred years ago moving around, going about their daily activities. It's usually easier for me to do that in a place like this, rather than in a structured environment like a "historic fort" or "living history museum", where staff in period costume try to stay in character for the tourists. I know they are well-intentioned and they're working hard, but it just seems easier to me the other way.

The Turquoise Trail was quiet and rural; all along the road, you see the iconic dusty western town that is so familiar from the movies. One thing you won't find is a lot of gas stations. Not a one, I don't think, so be prepared. You will see trading posts, Tinkertown and other museums, art galleries and mines where beautiful turquoise of many different sorts is found.

Cerrillos turquoise, light, medium—I saw numerous colors and types. Turquoise is the New Mexico state gem, and the U.S. is the world's largest producer of this gemstone. I saw about a hundred pieces I'd love to have.

In Santa Fe, the acquisitive urge became almost overwhelming. It is the city of art, and the paintings in the galleries seemed all to be calling my name. Finally, in self-defense, I invented a game and gave myself an imaginary budget. Every time I saw a canvas and knew which wall I'd put it on, I noted the price, added it to my shipping list, and imagined receiving it at home. The budget ceiling was very quickly crashed but that was alright. By the end of the afternoon I had invested eighty thousand imaginary dollars.

The art districts of the city were easy to find, and the galleries so charming they almost seemed like works of art themselves. I loved the flowers planted to curl up the walls and the hidden gardens and groves.

Santa Fe is famous for many things and one of them is the artist Georgia O'Keeffe. There is a large museum with a research center, and the galleries there make a great introduction to her art or a place to go if you already admire her work, and want to pay homage. Opened twenty years ago, the museum has collections of three thousand of her pieces and maintains her two homes and studios in northern New Mexico.

The weather had warmed up since our New Mexico drive began and it was steaming hot. I'd been warned to pace myself through Santa Fe, as the heat and the altitude can drain a person of energy. The city is seven thousand feet above sea level—that's almost twice as high as the highest peak in Vermont! Some people talk about and experience 'altitude sickness' (nausea, loss of appetite, fatigue), but in my case the effects of the altitude showed up as a powerful wish for a nice, frosty glass of beer.

We stumbled into the oldest restaurant in New Mexico by accident. El Farol has been serving small plates since 1835! And I suppose that's proof again that it's very difficult to come up with an idea that is truly new. It is a quiet place with an outdoor patio and an indoor bar that displays an amazing selection of bottles—far too many to count. A dance floor dominated one end of the room, and I was told that flamenco dancing would be part of the entertainment that evening.

I wanted to go, I really did, but by the end of the day, at seven thousand feet and after spending eighty thousand imaginary dollars on art, I was exhausted. Again, next time.

The imaginary art budget (and the non-existent fund for art) turned out to be a good idea. It was one I will use again, if I ever go to the biggest city in this next state—however, on this road trip I was headed for the smaller cities and the quieter places, off the Interstate.

Chapter Seventeen

NEW YORK

New York is a state where I have done the return trip for "next time" many times. The City itself is one of the wonders of the world, and the places beyond NYC are numerous and captivating.

Upstate New York has almost as many different regions as New York City has boroughs. The roads I traveled for this book ran from Buffalo in the northwest of the state to Saratoga Springs and then north through the Adirondack Mountains to Plattsburgh, near the northeast corner of the state. I pictured the route as a large, backward-facing L, starting at the bottom left.

The first part of the road trip wasn't, technically, "off the Interstate". I decided on I-90, from Buffalo through to Syracuse, for the usual time-management reasons. It runs just north of the Finger Lakes—wine and vacation country.

The scenery was stupendous. It's a beautiful agricultural area and was just lovely in June when we traveled through.

They get big storms and blizzards through here, though. We passed a Department of Transport yard with snowplows lined up. One large one had a sign across its plow— "115 inches of snow annually"!

New York seemed to have numerous roadside stops and travel centers. I found the rest of my state magnets here. For about fifteen years I've been collecting magnets from the states I've visited. The pace has picked up dramatically in the past four years, and now I've been to almost all of them. But I had only found about twenty of the magnets and the magnetic map of the U.S. that I bought to display them had a lot of gaps. Until New York. The first travel center where we stopped had almost everything I needed and the second had all the pieces required to finish off the collection. I left out Nebraska because I hadn't been there yet, but I know where to go to get it, if I can't find it while I'm there.

Collecting is an interesting thing, psychologically. I know many people who collect, everything from spoons to skeins of yarn to jewelry to posters to clothing to books. It's a way of documenting, I think. Photographs do that, so do journals, even playlists, but somehow there is something about acquiring an object and linking it to a time, a place, an experience, that is different. Of course, some people don't have this urge at all but for someone like me, who has it big-time . . . well, it's a good thing I decided on magnets and mugs rather than pianos or cars, or we'd be living in a box in the back yard while the collection filled every inch of available indoor space!

Just west of Syracuse, I encountered signs commemorating Harriet Tubman and the Underground Railroad. After the Civil War ended, she moved to New York, establishing many ties and doing much good work in the region near Auburn, just north of Owasco Lake. Harriet Tubman was born into slavery and after escaping in 1849 and finding freedom in Pennsylvania, she became one of the 'conductors' on the Underground Railroad, guiding many people to safety. During the Civil War, she worked on the Union Side, as a nurse and a scout, and became the first woman in American history to lead an armed raid, in 1863. After the war, she continued her efforts for equality and dignity, helping to set up schools for freed slaves, building a care home for the aged in Auburn, and fighting for voting rights for all. Harriet Tubman National Historical Park is open to the public in Auburn, near where she is buried.

As we got closer to Syracuse, I started to notice a lot of Italian and classical names. Rome, Ithaca, Utica, Syracuse. There was a Battle of Syracuse in 415 BC and there's a Syracuse, Sicily that is also heavy into the salt industry as this area is. I think the salt was the reason for the choice of name.

I have a page (actually, pages) of names of places that impressed me, even in ten seconds passing by at sixty mph, and that I'd like to revisit. Lake Onandaga, one of the gems of this region, is on the list. It's a very pretty area just east of Syracuse, near the Little Falls exit.

The landscape was showing more rolling hills now and was becoming more expansive somehow. The eye candy was green meadows, sparkling lakes, and thousands of trees. All very green and beautiful that day, but I'll bet it's amazing in October in fall foliage season.

Saratoga Springs was the destination for this day, and the reason we'd passed by some of the other intriguing or stunning spots. I'd been reading and hearing about the Saratoga Springs Race Course for years and I wanted to see it for myself. Racing season had not yet begun, but I was interested just to see the buildings. It dates back one hundred fifty-five years, to 1863, and is the scene of the Travers Stakes, the Hopeful Stakes, and Carly Simon's comment to the unnamed listener in "You're So Vain", that his horse "naturally won."

We drove past the gates in midafternoon, and it was completely easy to drive in to the grounds. I saw the gazebo that is part of the Saratoga logo, the three tracks that make up the race course grounds, the Big Red Spring, and the path that leads from the stables through the picnic grounds to the paddock prior to each race.

All around the town, on street corners, outside historic hotels and pubs, I was snapping photos of statues of horses, some painted horse colors and some painted in elaborate and vivid styles. Even in the hotel lobby, the horse world and culture were evident everywhere, with miniatures on the tabletops, and drawings and paintings on the walls.

We walked to lunch at the Old Bryan Inn, established in 1773 at 123 Maple Street. The history of the location is interwoven with lore about the healing properties of the nearby springs. The inn and restaurant are housed in a fascinating historic building that comes complete with reports from visitors about visions of ghosts—a woman in a green dress, a soldier in red, a horse and rider.

Some people love this idea (not me, particularly) and will count a vacation a good one if they've been on a ghost tour. No idea whether they say the same if they've actually seen a ghost.

After our stay in Saratoga Springs, it was time to go off the Interstate. We took Highway 9N, up toward the edge of Adirondack Park, past Glens Falls and Lake George. This is simply an incredibly beautiful area. Parts of the town of Lake George are quite kitschy but if I'm on vacation—hey, whatever. The scenery, the tiny roads through the trees, and the entire region itself were reason enough to be there.

Highway 9N meanders through quiet towns and past many stopping places for people enjoying the forest, the mountains and the water. The roads weren't in the best condition, and the car might have been protesting the lack of opportunity to take the curves at a spicier speed, but again, whatever. It was all good.

We drove north on the west side of Lake Champlain, which runs along the boundary between New York and Vermont, using 9N and then 22.

The roads were just incredibly gorgeous and scenic. It made me think of the car commercials on TV, showing the SUV conquering the twisty road, with mountains and lakes in the distance. I've often wondered—why won't they label those roads? I think we'd all like to know where they are. Or—maybe they are just CGI? Ad-agency photoshopping? Showing us Shangri-La for drivers—roads that don't really exist?

All too soon, we were arriving at the ferry landing near

Plattsburgh. It connects I-87 in New York and I-89 in Vermont, running every ten or fifteen minutes or so. It took us about fifteen minutes to cross, and like time on the water anywhere, those fifteen minutes felt like a two-week vacation.

By this point on the trip, I'd been through six regions of New York state: the area around Buffalo, near Canada; the one just south of Lake Ontario; the Finger Lakes; Saratoga Springs; the Adirondacks; and now the western edge of Lake Champlain. All beautiful and all distinct.

One thing I've wondered about for months (maybe years) is why the license plates in New York proclaim "Empire State". Oh, I do know it *is* the Empire state, but why and where did that come from? Turns out the phrase was a nickname that turned up on license plates in the fifties and sixties and then reappeared in the early twenty-first century (and by the way, New York was the first state to require drivers to license their vehicles, in 1901). Where did it come from? Some sources say it just grew organically from the image of New York being the state with wealth and many wealthy people; others point to a 1785 letter referring to it as the "seat of the Empire". Since the U.S. had already left the British Empire by that point, they must have been visualizing some sort of American Empire, yet to rise—or perhaps the letter writer hadn't yet got the memo about 1776.

Anyway, the Empire State it is, according to its twenty-first-century license plates. Nobody has officially questioned the phrase, unlike the situation in the state I traveled for the chapter coming up next.

Chapter Eighteen

OHIO

The Ohio license plate proclaims the state as the Birthplace of Aviation. Ohio was the victor in a battle with North Carolina over which state *was* the birthplace of aviation, awarded the title by Congress because the Wright brothers did all their early design work and built the first airplane prototypes in their bicycle shop there, before moving on to Kitty Hawk on the North Carolina Outer Banks for the early test flights.

Besides aviation, Ohio is known for the Rock 'n' Roll Hall of Fame in Cleveland. That's very famous, in my book. Oh yeah—this *is* my book. So there you go.

Our road trip to one of the side roads in Ohio took place in late September, when the corn was "as high as an elephant's eye". And yes, I know that song was from *Oklahoma*, but there is a lot of corn in Ohio, too. We started at the border with Indiana and drove toward New Paris, a small town on Route 320, a two-lane road that meandered past farmhouses and groves of trees. The air was warm and full of good smells . . . harvest time. I think I smelled some onions, along the way. It's not quite as flat as some other areas in this region and I felt a few rolling hills under our wheels. I even saw a snow-tubing place called Valley's Edge. It was hard to imagine this land covered in snow, on a soft, late-summer day with everything so green.

We rode along for about twenty miles and didn't see another car. I saw a sign that pointed to a covered bridge, but we gave it a pass in favor of cruising on toward Greenville and having more time in the museum there.

The Garst Museum is located in a nineteenth-century house added to the National Register of Historic Places in 1977 and given by the Garst family for the use of the Darke County Historical Society. I picked up a brochure that said there are 300,000 artifacts in 13,000 square feet of exhibit space.

The ones I was most interested in had to do with veteran broadcaster Lowell Thomas. Lowell Thomas was an adventurer, author, and newscaster who hosted the first ever television news broadcast in 1939. The list of things he did first goes on and on, but he probably created the biggest stir of his career when he introduced Lawrence of Arabia to the American public, via news reports and film from what was at that time a mysterious and seldom-visited part of the world.

Lowell Thomas also wrote and published dozens of books and was a partner in the group that introduced the technology of Cinerama to American movie-goers.

He was born in Woodington, Ohio, and although his career took him far from Ohio the state still claims him as a native son and supports this excellent museum treatment of his life. The highlight is a continuously running film of one of the travelogues that he created, after his newscasting career was done.

Annie Oakley is the other famous person who comes from this part of Ohio, and she is also showcased in the Garst Museum. I remember seeing a movie called *Annie Get Your Gun* on late-night TV back in my babysitting days. She was a sharpshooter and trick rider who earned a job in Buffalo Bill Cody's Wild West Show back in a time when women were too busy bearing children and keeping them clean, fed, and clothed to do much else. Annie learned to shoot and ride as a child and worked throughout her life to hone her skills. She was an entertainer and was celebrated around the world, with African tribal chiefs wanting to bring her to their countries to help with security and European aristocrats competing with each other to have to her at their tables.

The museum also tells of the love affair between Annie and her husband, Frank Butler. The exhibit is bursting with items from their life and travels together. She never called herself Annie Butler and no one is quite sure where "Oakley" came from (although some accounts say that Frank gave it to her as a sort of stage name just because it sounded good).

Many stars have portrayed her in various formats: Bernadette Peters, Mary Martin, Ethel Merman, Doris Day. The museum has a lively display of Annie Oakley's appearances in popular culture long after her passing.

My favorite part of the exhibit was the use of some of the historic photographs of her time, including quite a startling picture of Annie lined up to shoot an apple off the head of her dog, sitting patiently on top of a stool. Now that's a well-trained, loyal dog.

The history of Greenville incudes much more than Lowell Thomas and Annie Oakley, of course. It was the site of the Greene Ville Treaty, signed in 1795 to end the fighting between the Native Americans, the settlers, and the soldiers in nearby Fort Green Ville. Among the hundreds of thousands of artifacts shown in this museum are more than a thousand Native American arrowheads, all carefully cataloged and displayed by era, dating back centuries.

The museum also contains a wonderful display of typical nineteenth-century Ohio life, with dining rooms, bedrooms, sitting rooms, and parlors fully furnished, and the interiors of a bank, a newspaper, a toy store, and other places of business painstakingly reconstructed. The final surprise, when I turned a corner near the end of the building, was a large room filled with the history of transportation. A penny-farthing bicycle, labeled 1812, antique motorcycles, carriages and carts that were once pulled by horses, and even three sleighs.

The whole place was a delight, but I'd have to say my favorite item in the museum was a painting of Annie Oakley, riding a horse at top speed. She is bent from the waist, leaning backward toward the horse's rump, but slightly to her right to reach down to the ground. No reins, no hands, just knees controlling the horse. According to the exhibit information, it was also one of her favorites, of thousands of paintings and photographs done of her.

The image conveyed a sense of joy and exuberance. Those emotions, plus Annie's trick-riding position in the painting, reminded me of one of the way that sailors lean way out over the side of a boat (an action called hiking), using their weight to balance it when it is heeled over, pulled to one side by the force of the wind in the sails. Sailors, sailboats, and people riding the wind are a sight you'd see frequently in
the state in focus in the next chapter

Chapter Nineteen

RHODE ISLAND

Hiking in sailing—leaning out over the water to use your weight to counteract the heeling (leaning) action of the boat—looks a lot like trick riding. It's a sight you'd see a lot, at the right time, on Narragansett Bay, Rhode Island.

When we set out to see Rhode Island, on a road trip from Vermont, I mapped out a route that would include the state capital of Providence, as well as the towns of Newport and Narragansett. All are relatively small places, and Rhode Island is the smallest of the states, in land mass, and one of the largest, in international reputation. For more than fifty years, from 1930 to the early eighties, the historic seaside town of Newport was host to the most important event in yacht racing, the America's Cup. The nearby islands of Martha's Vineyard, Chappaquiddick, and Nantucket have been made famous by politicians, pop singers, and limerick writers; and the legendary inhabitants of that other Camelot, Jackie and John F. Kennedy, got married there in 1953.

It was an easy day trip from Stowe. Even with stops to enjoy the White Mountains in New Hampshire, we were cruising past Boston by early afternoon. This city has some of the thickest, fastest, and most unpredictable traffic I've seen so far in the U.S. But the ring road let us avoid the really busy areas downtown and near the river, despite the best efforts of our GPS to direct us that way. Boston is a lot of fun, and I was looking forward to being back there one day, but not on this trip. We took the Interstates around the outskirts of the city then hopped on Highway 24 to head south toward Newport.

I got us a bit lost heading down the peninsula toward Newport, and we sidetracked into Portsmouth, a lovely place with many modern examples of that classic New England–style of architecture: square-shaped houses covered in cedar shingles, weathered to a vintage look. But it wasn't what I'd come to see, so we found our way back to the right road (which turned out to be Highway 138) and carried on into Newport.

You know how some people that you see on the streets of some cities just look like they belong there? If you were to play a guessing game, with no maps, no GPS, and no other information but the people and the buildings, where would you be? (And if you see a sign that says New York's Best Desserts you have to disqualify yourself.)

In Newport, within thirty seconds I saw a dozen people who looked as though they'd be totally comfortable sailing around the world in an open sailboat. Tanned, tight skin, long hair in various shades from brown to red to white, practical clothes, boat shoes. We passed a laundromat that advertised special rates for sailing laundry, restaurants that offered every kind of seafood imaginable cooked in every kind of way, and then a waterfront that was a visual delight for anyone who likes ships and the sea. We stopped for some refreshment at a pub called The Fastnet, a term that confused me because I would have thought that to catch a lot of fish that way you'd want to dip or drag your net slowly. But perhaps I am too literal . . . or perhaps it wasn't fish they were thinking of when they named it.

Okay, I did some research and it turns out the Fastnet Pub is an Irish gathering place in Newport. Fastnet Rock in the UK lent its name to a famous sailing race. Sailing, not fishing.

From there we walked around the historic district, checking out buildings that dated back to the 1670s. It was just fascinating to imagine something standing for nearly three hundred and fifty years. Many of the streets are very narrow and it was easy to visualize them, back in the day, crowded with pedestrians and maybe the occasional horse, rather than tourists, taxis, and minivans.

I've spent quite a bit of time exploring Savannah and Charleston, and I'd say this town easily matches those beautiful places for historic significance, painterly charm, and nautical atmosphere. Besides the historic homes and businesses, you've got the cobblestone wharves, filled with places to shop, eat, and socialize. You've got Cliff Walk, a 3.5-mile trail that edges on some of the most beautiful coastal scenery in all of New England. You've got the Newport Mansions on Bellevue Avenue (think Astors, Vanderbilts, *Great Gatsby*). There are ten or so of them, some open to the public for tours (not on my to-do list). These were the summer cottages of some of America's wealthiest people during what they called the Gilded Age, after the American Civil War and before World War I, and most were used for only six weeks in summer, during "the season".

We also drove around Ocean Drive, also known as Ten Mile Drive, or just The Drive. More mansions, with glorious views and extensive grounds, plus some secluded beaches, are the appeal here.

Newport is also the scene of the Newport Jazz Festival and the Newport Folk Festival, both famous and both good reasons to return one day.

I was there in late summer on a misty, chilly day. It was perfect for feeling the ocean ambiance but I imagine it's quite different in high summer, with the beaches filled with families, couples, and friends having their playtime.

Next, the road led us across a bridge and onward to Highway 4, toward Providence. Providence is where you go to find a more urban feel, and its hotels are the launching point for many of the tours that go off to Martha's Vineyard and Nantucket. We decided to go for the 'fine dining experience'—including a wine pairing—where you choose what you want to eat and the restaurant chooses what you'll have to drink with it. I agreed to this, but the first thing they brought me as a "wine pairing" was sherry . . . which, I get it, technically *is* wine (actually fortified wine, and can get you tipsy faster than regular wine) but what I had in mind to go with my lovely cheese plate was something crisp, chilled, and white. I was stuck on the etiquette at this point. What do you do if you don't like their "pairing"? Will the waiter be insulted? Is he the one who chose this sherry? If he is insulted, will my main course ever arrive?

As it turned out, he was quite easygoing about it. He did explain to me why the sherry was a good choice but took it away anyway.

The next day we turned south once again to double back on the road we'd seen very briefly, between Narragansett and Providence. Narragansett is the site of a famous architectural feature called The Towers, all that is left of a casino built on the pier in the 1880s. The Calamari Festival was in full swing as I passed through (also, not on my to-do list). We drove the road right out to the end, at Point Judith lighthouse; from there I could stare out to sea. The waves were high and gray—in fact, the sky, the beach sand, the water, everything looked gray and misty. The air was salty and all stirred up; there was quite a stiff breeze. All I was missing was a boat.

I loved the waves off Rhode Island and the views from its shore. Coastline is one of the most beautiful sights anywhere, a geographic quality the Ocean State has in common with the place in the next chapter.

Chapter Twenty

SOUTH CAROLINA

About nine hundred miles farther down the U.S. East Coast, you see South Carolina. Its nickname is The Palmetto State and when I first drove there, it seemed as though those trees were *everywhere*. Palmettos, plus salt marsh, brilliant sunshine, and warm air. The palmetto tree is also on the state flag, in white on an indigo background with a crescent moon above it. Apparently, the iconography and colors of the flag came from various elements of the uniforms of soldiers fighting the British in the 1770s. It's one more example of how much American symbolism and visual identity come from war experiences.

What's the difference between a palmetto and a palm? Height, mainly (palmettos grow to thirty feet, palm trees as high as eighty), and perspective: palms go vertical and palmettos grow horizontally, sometimes below ground.

As we traveled through Savannah, heading for the bridge that leads north into South Carolina (a concept that it took me several months to get my head around), I saw many license plates with the palmetto and crescent moon. The new plates also have the state motto, translated from the Latin, written across the top: *While I Breathe I Hope*.

The origins of South Carolina's association with this phrase go back to 1776 and probably have something to do with a war (as does New Hampshire's bit of license plate philosophy, *Live Free or Die*).

On this road trip I was looking for a break in the heat. South Carolina, along with all of the other Southern states, gets mad-hot in the summer. From May to October, really, I was seeing and feeling temperatures from the mid-80s to the mid-90s. I had stopped looking at the "Feels Like" slot on my phone's weather app because it invariably added another ten degrees to the temperature.

Our destination that day was Charleston, the largest city in South Carolina. (The capital city is Columbia.) We could get there by starting on the Interstate, I-95, and then slowing down and coming into town on Highway 17. That's a good choice if y'all want to be there in under two hours. But I-95 doesn't really offer much to see—unless you're bypassing Charleston and heading north to North Carolina, where just before the state line you come to a theme park called "South of the Border". It almost can't be described. The first time I saw it, I was approaching from North Carolina, and I swear that about sixty miles before we got to the turn-off, the billboards started shouting at me from the roadside. I can only imagine what it's like to go through there with a carful of kids—an hour or more of reading billboards, begging to stop, and asking "are we there yet?" Pedroland, the Reptile Lagoon, and the Sombrero Tower . . .I could even get married South of the Border. If I wanted to.

That's all if you are driving south to South Carolina but this time I was going north, off the Interstate, on Highway 17 to check out some of the towns, cities, and islands along the way to Charleston.

It is not difficult to find smaller roads off the Interstate in South Carolina. The area to the east of I-95 is a web of asphalt, spun out from freeway running north and south through the center of the state like Charlotte the spider going nuts. You could explore for weeks, even months, I think, especially on a motorbike.

The road conditions aren't great, though, I have to say. In fact, South Carolina has become our go-to comparison, whenever we encounter potholes and washboard roads anywhere. "It's like being back in South Carolina."

Out of Savannah we took the road to the town of Bluffton. This is so close that it's almost a suburb of Savannah (except for being in a different state and all). US 17N, then SC 315 and SC 46 took us across salt marshes and under pine trees toward a charming town with a complex history. The Lowcountry was the cradle for separatist sentiment as far back as the mid-eighteenth century and it was the first state to side against the Union in the Civil War.

Many of the historic homes of that and even earlier days have been preserved and are open to the public. The beautiful May River is another reason to go there. We stopped for a picnic and a walk around the dock, but then hurried back to the car. I wanted to zigzag around quite a few of the barrier islands, take a look at Myrtle Beach, then end up in Charleston before nightfall, and it was an ambitious itinerary.

Very ambitious, as it turned out. Even though I had planned a long, full day trip from Savannah, with random, spontaneous stops along the way, following my nose, essentially, there were some practical limits to my curiosity. Myrtle Beach, one of the biggest and most popular vacation areas on the Atlantic coast, is ninety-five miles *north* of Charleston and it would have been just too far to go in one day. I do have a habit of doing this, planning trips that would involve gobbling up miles like a good vacuum cleaner facing a dust bunny bonanza: I can only plead guilty to geographic optimism and research avoidance.

After Bluffton, I wanted to see Hilton Head Island. This spot is well known, even up into remote parts of Canada, as a mecca for talented young golfers. On the way into the center of town, I stopped counting after about the hundredth chain store or restaurant—it's mile after mile of suburban plaza. On both sides of the street. Hilton Head itself is quite pretty, with a picturesque lighthouse and some nice places to have lunch on the waterfront.

From Hilton Head it was on to Beaufort, by way of Highway SC 170E. This is a really walkable small city, with galleries and restaurants every few feet. It's also the location of the mansion used in the eighties movie *The Big Chill* and we had to do a pass by there, just to take a look. The house was under serious renovation and reconstruction at the time.

Beaufort is also very close by St. Helena Island, an important place for Gullah culture and home to the Penn Center, which is an outstanding examination of the contributions of African Americans to the area.

By the way, have I mentioned that the correct pronunciation of Beaufort is Byou' - fert? Have you been pronouncing it in your head the French way, Bo - for'?

It is one place name that I had to practice. Wilkes-Barre, Pennsylvania is another; I would have thought Wilkes Bar, not Wilkesburry. And Worcester, Massachusetts, which is Wooster, not War-kester. Or Peabody, Massachusetts. It's Pee-b'dee, if you don't want to sound like an out-of-towner. For Billerica (does not rhyme with America), same thing. (but it's Billrika, not Billeryeka).

After a very nice Southern lunch in Beaufort, we drove north toward the beach areas to find some places to try to walk it off. It would be a short walk, because we had more ground to cover. You've got about seventy miles via Highway 17 between Beaufort and Charleston, but in between I also wanted to see Edisto Beach, Edisto Island, Kiawah Island, and Folly Beach. Perhaps we could also get a little farther north, too, to Isle of Palms—all places that we've heard Charleston friends recommend.

One of the things I couldn't miss, passing through this area, was the large number of churches. Seemed like every few hundred yards, there was another one. We've been through the area on Sundays, too, and the church parking lots are just packed, many of the larger ones (in several cities in several states, not just South Carolina) requiring police directing traffic as the vehicles go in and out of the church grounds.

The beach areas along the way were just as glorious as advertised. White sand, blue-gray ocean, dunes, sea grass—my camera was pretty much permanently raised to my right eye.

Coming into Charleston, I was enchanted by . . . well, just everything. The Ashley and the Cooper rivers, the waterfront, the historic buildings. We parked near the Battery and walked along, looking out toward Fort Sumter where the Civil War began. Across from the water a lovely park provided shade and food for thought, as I looked around an area that had been in active use for hundreds and hundreds of years. The walk continued up and down the streets lined with amazing historic homes.

Charleston and Savannah are both historic and beautifully preserved. Savannah had more of an 'everyday' atmosphere, as a place where people live and work, with some tourism on the side. Charleston seemed, to me, more like a place for visitors—but perhaps that's because I lived in the first city and was a visitor in the second.

South Carolina gives a gentle, easy vibe, and if you're in a big hurry here you're going to stick out like a two-year-old on bingo night in an old folks' home. And why rush, anyway? Especially when it's ninety-five degrees, and feels like a hundred and one?

The end of our day trip between Savannah and Charleston brought us back on Highway 17, a little more directly than on the way north, at the beginning of the day. I'd seen a lot of historic buildings and water views, and met many people very proud of their home state.

I had also seen a lot of golf courses. South Carolina has more than three hundred of them, apparently, which puts it right up there in the group of states with the most.

It is also home to thousands of mini-golf courses, with Myrtle Beach claiming about fifty of them along its Grand Strand. (I don't know whether South Carolina has "the most" mini-golf courses; all I could find were a lot of places that claimed "the best".) North Carolina is one of the states that claims "the first golf course", competing for that title with the state I focused on for the next chapter.

Chapter Twenty-One

TENNESSEE

Chattanooga, TN is the city that claims to be the location of the first mini-golf course in America, and if we add the word "patented", I think they might be right. Pinehurst, North Carolina had one earlier, in 1916, (called "Thistle Dhu") but the idea was patented in 1927 in Tennessee at Lookout Mountain resort.

On previous trips to the state, I've been to Nashville and to Chattanooga, and I'm sure there are many other wonderful places to explore in Tennessee, but I really wanted to get to Memphis, so there you are. Memphis, one of the homes of the Blues. Also the home of Graceland and all things Elvis.

I had been humming the great Marc Cohn song "Walking in Memphis" ever since I first heard it about ten years ago and now I had a chance to get "my feet ten feet off of Beale".

Beale Street is famous in music world. Not Sarah Palin famous but George Washington or Martin Luther King Jr. famous. We stayed in a hotel on Main Street, a short distance from Beale. When I arrived that September day, it was sunny and warm in Memphis, so different from what was south and east of us in Florida with Hurricane Irma.

We walked Main Street toward Beale, crossed Union Avenue, then Monroe, and saw the Orpheum sign, a facade on an ugly building. Elvis Presley Park commanded the next corner. Then I hung a left onto Beale Street, and took a photo of the marker. The sign tells the story of the first schools for "freedmen" in 1866.

The street was jumping with lively bars and restaurants. B.B. King's, Alfred's, Rum Boogie Café, Blues Hall, Silky O'Sullivan's. We had lunch at Silky O'Sullivan's on an outdoor patio with live music filling the warm Southern air around us. I heard "What a Wonderful World", "Mr. Bojangles", and "Give Me One Reason to Stay Here". Hah! In half an hour I'd seen a dozen reasons.

They also have Irish drinking goats at Silky O'Sullivan's that allegedly come down a slide (alleged by the restaurant's advertising). I didn't see it, but that's not to say it didn't happen. I just didn't stay (and drink) long enough.

The patio had autographs in the concrete, with many famous names joining us for lunch. We sat by Johnny Cash's square. Indoors there was a very cool saloon, two pianos, and a long bar.

After a very filling lunch we walked along the street, where the sidewalk had copper music notes embedded in the concrete sidewalk with famous musicians' names beneath them. The street also had W.C. Handy's Memphis house, moved here from its original location and now a museum.

Our walk carried us about a fifteen-minute distance to the Blues Museum and then past the Civil Rights Museum, at the Lorraine Motel where Martin Luther King Jr. was shot in April of 1968. I stood in front of it for a long while, wondering how things might have been different if he'd lived.

After some heavy moments, we walked on to the Peabody Hotel, famous for its ducks. Change of pace, change of plan.

I've seen these ducks before and they are a kick. They live upstairs on the rooftop but every morning they are brought down in an elevator to a large, marble fountain and pond in the lobby where they float around all day and entertain the tourists.

Then at 5 p.m. they're escorted back to their residence upstairs, by a 'keeper' dressed in red livery as if he is prepared to be stationed by the front entrance to open the door for important guests.

The Peabody has been at this location since 1925 and the duck tradition began in the early thirties. The hotel and lobby are luxurious and grand; somehow the contrast of ducks is just whimsical enough.

We had dinner at Flight on the Main Street Mall. I'd seen flights of beer, small glasses of three different types to try, and flights of wine, but this restaurant took it into food. Salads, three of each to try. Main courses, appetizers, deserts. Too much food and portions too big—that's the case everywhere in the South. You need the metabolism of a cheetah.

We walked back along Main Street at 8 p.m. and there were very few people around. But when we got to Beale Street I realized that that's where they all were.

We settled in to listen to the music at B.B. King's, where the first act was Memphis Jones, a long-haired guy who introduced himself as a "professional rock and roll historian". He showed a lot of joy in his playing. The second act was the B.B. King All-Stars, seven or eight pieces, with a trumpet player, drummer, keyboard player, singer, and guitarists. Just outstanding.

Afterward we walked Beale Street after dark. It was all lit up with neon and I really felt as though I were walking in a place that just resonated with history.

On a previous trip I'd seen Sun Records and Graceland and didn't feel any urge to repeat the tours. I only have capacity for a certain amount of playing tourist. But maybe next time I visit again, I'll hit 're-fresh' on those places.

Also, next time, I'd like to stay at the Peabody. Wildlife that lives indoors. You don't see that every day.

I enjoy seeing wildlife anywhere, any time. I thought my odds were fairly high in the wide, open spaces of the state in the next chapter.

Chapter Twenty-Two

TEXAS

While there certainly is a lot of open space in Texas, there is a lot of city space, too. If you drive just the big cities, you see a lot of concrete. In fact, going "off the Interstate" probably gives more contrast in Texas than in any other state, except perhaps California. Ironic because the primary image of Texas is not concrete, it's cowboys on the open range. But off the Interstate you will see the wide-open spaces (and in a way, the eight-lane highway itself feels like a wide-open space).

The other image of Texas, of course, is oil. Whether by the Interstate or on the side roads, you see a lot of drilling.

For this drive to see clients, in winter of 2018, we traveled from Plano to the outskirts of Dallas to Fort Worth (a distance of about fifty miles) and then onto 281 for about a hundred and fifty miles to Lampasas and then on 183 for about forty-five into Austin.

I've done a few other drives in the Lone Star state. I know the lone star refers to the flag, but whenever I see or hear the reference I always think "lonely star" because somehow the vastness of some of the wilder regions of the state just hollers 'lonesome'. Highway 273 through El Paso, for example. I was anxious to see that city because when I was a kid, the song "El Paso" was played constantly on the radio, in Edmonton, Alberta.

The list of cultural references to Texas places is a long one. Paris, Texas, the "second largest Paris in the world" was the setting for a movie, and Del Rio, Texas, the filming location for TV series *Lonesome Dove*. Thanks to Wim Wenders, Larry McMurtry and a few others, most of us have quite a bit of imagery associated with Texas.

Jimmy Webb and Glenn Campbell gave us the song "Galveston". One of my uncles was stationed at a naval base there during World War II, and that was another reason I had some curiosity about the city. I had visited there on a previous day trip out of Houston, and Galveston turned out to be a lovely seaside place, somewhat beaten down by Hurricane Ike in 2009 but still vibrant, particularly in the area near the pier.

This trip we started off in the suburb of Plano, where I saw a herd of Texas longhorn cattle statues, fake-galloping along a street median with heavy traffic on either side. The Plano-Dallas-Fort Worth area contains a lot of cars . . . a *lot*. It was quite a boring drive, with nothing but the back ends of other cars and the undersides of massive trucks to look at. I amused myself by looking for the license plates that read "Don't Mess with Texas". That one is right up there with two of my favorite slogans: "Maine: The Way Life Should Be" (which means what, exactly?) and "A Great Place to Live for Many Reasons" (signs of a mission statement planning meeting gone horribly wrong).

Once we reached Highway 281 we left the dense traffic behind. It's the longest scenic road in Texas, running from the Oklahoma line down to the Mexican border. Most of the segment we drove was two-lane road, with typical towns all along the way. The timing wasn't right for us to stop for a meal, but if we'd been looking, we would have chosen the Koffee Kup, a legendary spot in Hico that draws many local people and where the motto is "Pie Fixes Everything". In Lampasas, it's Storm's, where "It's About the Burger".

At Lampasas we scooted over to Austin on 183. Austin is a place I'd visit over and over again. We checked into a downtown hotel, road-weary and ready for some stationary time. From the window, I watched the river and the bridge. Bats live under the bridge and sleep all day. When night falls, they fly out by the thousands. People line the riverbanks and go out in boats to see the sight.

Austin also has numerous terrific Tex-Mex restaurants and the South Congress neighborhood, which is just so much fun to just stroll around and explore. Locals have been proud to be "weird" for decades and the inclination has been nailed down in a phrase you see on bumper stickers, T-shirts and posters: "Keep Austin Weird".

Austin is home to the South by Southwest Festival, which is growing in importance to the entertainment, innovation, and other industries every year, and the Austin Film Festival, neither of which was on when I was there. Maybe another time. It is also home to dozens if not hundreds of live music venues. Many music pros make Austin their home and many out-of-towners go there in October to be part of the tapings for the TV series *Austin City Limits* live concerts, broadcast on PBS.

Now there's an example of the power of the screen to romanticize a place! In the same category, but on the big screen, we have the movie associated with the state coming up in the next chapter.

Chapter Twenty-Three

VERMONT

When I was a girl, *The Sound of Music* was one of my favorite musicals. Based on a true story, it tells of Maria, the young girl who healed the von Trapp family and led them to safety across the Alps as the Nazis marched in to occupy Austria. I'd always wondered what became of them, and it turns out there is a valley in Vermont that they reached in 1939 and made their home.

It wasn't a unique discovery, and judging by the buses in the parking lot of the Trapp Family Lodge near Stowe, it's something that a lot of tourists have known about for quite some time. The family built a career as a singing group and as hotel proprietors, later branching out into agriculture, beer-making, and concert promotion, with a program of performances staged in the summer, in a meadow high in the Green Mountains.

It is a glorious spot that is very reminiscent of the opening scene of the musical and of Julie Andrews's voice soaring over the Alps. I saw it that first time in autumn, when the leaves on the trees were intense colors of red, orange, and yellow, but I can imagine that it is just as impressive, covered in four feet of snow.

We arrived at the lodge from a side road near Highway 108; the way was clearly marked. It was the end of a long morning of driving from Boston and the restaurant at the lodge seemed very inviting, yet it was difficult to tear myself away from the mountain view.

Difficult but not impossible. White wine and Mount Alice cheese beckoned.

The young waiter was dressed in warm clothing that looked quite European and Alpine. When I complimented him on the outfit, though, I thought I could read on his face that charm and character were fighting a losing battle against heat and discomfort.

"Warm?" I asked.

He nodded.

"I wouldn't have thought it would be this warm in Vermont in late September," I said.

"It changes, year to year," he said as he handed out the menus. "Some years there can be a hard rain day and then freezing in early September, other years not till stick season."

The six seasons in Vermont are: spring (when the red clover and other flowers bloom), summer (when you eat creemees and Ben and Jerry's ice cream), fall foliage (when the numbers of gold or ruby leaves are only outnumbered by the numbers of tourists), stick (when the leaves have all fallen from the trees), winter (when the cold weather and the blizzards come), and mud (self-explanatory).

This first road trip to Vermont had brought us from Boston up to Burlington, on the eastern shore of Lake Champlain. We stayed right across the street from the lakeshore, and the sunsets were absolutely intense, as vivid as any I saw in Hawaii.

We were there just at the beginning of fall foliage season, when the side roads and small highways in Vermont, New York, New Hampshire and Maine are crammed with "leaf peepers" as the locals and the tourist brochures call us. These are the people taking an escape weekend road trip to get away from sidewalks and concrete buildings into a landscape defined by trees. Driving through is wonderful; parking the car and hiking through is a whole other level higher.

Back on Highway 108, we headed toward Mount Mansfield, the highest peak in Vermont and the site of some epic skiing and snowboarding. For a small charge we drove the Toll Road up the mountainside and saw the valley from the summit. The view was sensational.

Back on the highway, the Zig pointed us toward Smugglers Notch, a section of highway that is completely closed during the winter months. Trees in full autumn color squeezed the road, and gradually it shrank from two lanes to one and a half, then eventually to barely a single lane, as he steered us around the twists and turns, then through the Notch.

Most of Smugglers Notch is in Mount Mansfield National Park. It got its name in the early 1800s when President Jefferson tried to keep America out of the Napoleonic Wars by preventing trade with Great Britain and with Canada. The Notch's story as a secret transportation route gained a new chapter in the 1850s and 1860s when fugitive slaves used it to escape to Canada. In the Roaring Twenties during the Prohibition era in the United States, "importers" would go to Canada to buy alcohol, bringing it back to sell in speakeasies and at private parties all over New England.

The mountain pass twists and turns through the forest; at the narrowest point only one vehicle can pass through at a time. Everyone was very cautious and courteous, and I was very appreciative. On the other side of the Notch, we stopped at a parking area that served hikers heading for this section of The Long Trail, a route that runs the length of Vermont and pre-dates the Appalachian Trail. Among the vehicles, there was a farm truck and a woman selling Vermont maple syrup. Well, who would say no? I picked up a two-quart jug that served us for six months after we got home.

It was a hot day, and I was happy to have the air-conditioning on in the car. They do get occasional heat waves here but very few of the houses are fully air-conditioned. It's like they believe it doesn't get hot here and when you see the photos of the buildings and village streets covered in snow, it's easy to see how they forget summer, once it's passed.

After the drive through the Notch, we circled back down on Highway 15, then took Highway 100 into the village of Stowe. It was like one of the postcard pictures of a New England town, with the white church in the middle of town: the river and the mountain valley beyond, with red, orange, and gold trees all around. Just a mile or so from town, we found a short, single-lane covered bridge. Apparently it dates back to 1844 and is known as Gold Brook Bridge, Stowe Hollow Bridge, or, most famously, Emily's Bridge. It was said to be named for a young woman whose ghost still waits there for a young man to return, according to one story. Another has it that she was jilted at the altar on her wedding day and died in a horses-and-wagon accident at the bridge after driving there, furious and determined to find him, then taking a corner too fast. There's another story that the first mention of "Emily" and anything haunted turned up in a high school student's paper in the late sixties. Hmmm. There have been quite a few reports of paranormal sightings and experiences; most of them seem to show that Emily is still annoyed.

I didn't see or feel anything, and we drove through *very* slowly. Not in the middle of the night, though.

Well, would you?

I saw hundreds of red barns along the roadsides of Highways 100 and Highway 108 and the valleys around them; Red Barn is also the name of many of the small businesses in the area and is part of the house design style. Farm animals are another frequent feature, with paintings of cows and roosters almost as frequently seen as the real live variety.

Vermont is incredibly beautiful with rolling hillsides, pretty roads, green mountains, rivers, wildflowers, and ponds around every bend. It was tempting to just follow the tiny side roads wherever they led, although one shopkeeper warned me that it was wise not to trust GPS in Vermont, because you never knew where you might end up. She said she had one friend who was directed, turn by turn, to an address she'd put in, and found herself looking at an ancient tree and hearing "You have arrived".

And what if it were the middle of the night and you followed the GPS, turn by turn, and ended up on Emily's Bridge, just in time to find out you'd done something to tick her off?

Vermont is the least populated of all fifty states, a fact that surprised me. Among its famous previous residents I found information about poet Robert Frost, eighteenth-century American revolutionary leader Ethan Allen, and the thirtieth U.S. president, Calvin Coolidge.

In the state featured in the next chapter, it is the third U.S. president, Thomas Jefferson, everywhere, all day long.

Chapter Twenty-Four

VIRGINIA

We set out to drive from Manassas to Monticello on a sunny late October day. When I was planning the trip and looking at the map, I was sold on the idea that this would be a sort of drive backward in time, from the scene of one of the most famous battles of the Civil War in the nineteenth century (better known in some circles as Bull Run) to the home built in the eighteenth century by the author of the Declaration of Independence, Thomas Jefferson.

To get to Monticello, the home he designed and built, we went off Interstate 64 East to Charlottesville, then Route 20 South and then Route 53 (also called the Thomas Jefferson Parkway). You won't mistake it for a quiet unpaved country road and a lot of people use it. Still, it *is* off the Interstate—and the chance to see a UNESCO World Heritage Site doesn't come along every day.

Actually, Monticello and the University of Virginia, also designed by Thomas Jefferson, together make up this World Heritage Site.

As we rolled along the two-lane blacktop, post-and-rail wood fencing lining the shoulders, I could see hillsides in the distance, covered with trees in full, fall glory, their outlines softly smudged, as in an Impressionist painting. There were just enough twists in the road to make it clear that it was a good idea to obey the double yellow, no-passing lines—but also enough twists to make me imagine that it would be lot of fun in a sports car or on a motorcycle. RV drivers should take their time.

We pulled off the road through a set of white gates and crept along a tree-lined driveway that was covered in fallen leaves. The parking lot was sizeable—no surprise that they get a lot of visitors here, I suppose.

Quite a few things about this house and about Thomas Jefferson impressed me, probably the most noteworthy being that he got started when he was only twenty-six. The name means "little mountain" in Italian, and its design is derived from Italian renaissance architectural principles. It sits on top of a small peak in the Southwest Mountains.

The grounds are equally impressive, and Jefferson has also been acknowledged for his skill and talent as a landscape architect. It was a beautiful spot, with a gorgeous view of the valley.

It's also obviously a very popular place, and we had to wait our turn to go on the bus up to the house. Popular with some residents of the insect world, too. Millions of ladybugs descended on all of us and hitched a ride right to the door of the mansion. We were all brushing them off shirts and pants as we hurried in through the front door.

The tour guide took us through the house, describing the origins of some of the furniture and other design features. The entry area is filled with unusual artifacts and gifts given to Jefferson and the place has the feel of a museum. Some of the stories of the restoration efforts were interesting; for example, technological advances enabled historians to identify the precise color of paint used in Jefferson's day and to replicate it on the walls of the dining room.

No photography is allowed inside the house, but there were many places to stop for photo ops on the grounds. The

West Portico steps, the tour guide told us, are chosen by many people, intent on getting that selfie in front of one of the most recognizable locations in the U.S., the image we've seen on coins and postage stamps, to name just a couple. They also frequently hold swearing-in ceremonies for new citizens on the Fourth of July.

Aerial photography is very rarely allowed; the airspace above Monticello is a no-fly zone. And leave your drone at home (same rule as at Churchill Downs).

Monticello was a 5,000-acre agricultural operation and hundreds of workers, black and white, toiled to build and maintain it. It was fascinating to see and to imagine life within those walls two hundred fifty years ago, but the place couldn't be experienced without a sense of the pain woven through its history, it seemed to me. What incredible irony that the Declaration of Independence was written by a man who owned people. Of course, there are many such paradoxes all over the world, and human history is crowded with cruelty and injustice. And with joy and kindness, yes, but sometimes you have to work hard to keep that in mind, when confronted with examples of the pain.

Monticello has made efforts to address the issue of the history of slave ownership, in Virginia and within its walls, and I'm not the one who can say whether they've done a good job. No one can undo what was done, all those centuries ago, but is it wrong to preserve places like Monticello for educational purposes?

But—where does education end and glorification begin?

From Monticello we could have driven west and explored Shenandoah National Park in the Blue Ridge Mountains; Skyline Drive is one of those 'have-to-do-someday' items on my list. But time did not permit this time, and I'll have to wait to find out how that drive compares with the one in my Top Ten, coming up in the state featured in the next (and last) chapter.

Chapter Twenty-Five

WASHINGTON

We were rolling along Route 20 through North Cascades National Park in Washington when the Zig came up with the idea for a TV show about cars.

Actually, I came up with it, but it was inspired by his comment about driving this rented Nissan through the mountains . . . that it was as if the car were dancing. Steering wheel turning, left, right, little bit left, again, a little bit more, then a hard right—absolutely, that's what it was like.

From there it was a short conversation to *Dancing with the Cars,* registering a domain name or two, and several weeks of discussion of structure (each contestant with a pro and an ordinary Joe on the team), roads (each week, one of the great U.S. driving challenge roads), and cars (classic? super?)

In the end, all it amounted to was an outline. We just didn't have enough interest or time to pursue it. But every time I see the TV ad with the dancing car I'm reminded of the TV show idea . . . and this great road that runs from I-5, east to Winthrop, Washington.

The great Pacific Northwest is a fantastic place to go, on foot or by car, if you enjoy towering fir trees, mountain vistas, ocean shores, and rain. Because you *will* see rain, lots of it, between October and May, in the fall, winter, and spring months. But this trip off the Interstate was on the calendar for late May and rain wasn't a consideration.

We started off early with nothing but coffee and orange juice and by lunch it was time to stop. Our destination was Sun Mountain Lodge, about a hundred sixty-five miles from I-5, using Highway 20. It bills itself as Washington's best destination resort, and not having been to all of them, I couldn't say. But it certainly was a good one, and the drive there was outstanding. Highway 20, also known as the North Cascades Highway, is part of the Cascade Loop, a four-hundred-mile tour through the mountain range. Avalanches often close the highway during winter months, and the Department of Transportation monitors it closely. It's usually closed for safety reasons from late November to early May.

The drive gave us incredible views of the Skagit River and of Lake Shannon. Once we were in North Cascades National Park, the visual feast was just nonstop. It would be impossible for me to pick a favorite spot but right up there would be Diablo Canyon and Diablo Lake, a reservoir formed by Diablo Dam. The lake is the color of the Caribbean Sea.

The Zig enjoyed the hairpin turn around the southern arm of the lake and the next leg of the road, on to Ross Lake. Then the highway crosses Rainy Pass, briefly joins the Pacific Crest Trail, climbs up into Chelan County, and then goes through Washington Pass, a sharp turn and down into eastern Washington.

A bit farther and we saw the Methow River, a tributary of the Columbia and the water feature nearest the town of Winthrop, our destination near the Lodge. Winthrop is a western-themed town and the story goes that author Owen Wister, a roommate of one of the town's leading citizens, came there to honeymoon, then wrote *The Virginian*, a famous 1902 western novel that became the basis of a very popular TV series broadcast in the sixties and seventies.

One of the funny things is that the novel is set in

Wyoming, about a man with no name called "The Virginian", written by a Massachusetts writer who dreamed it up while he was sitting in Washington state.

Winthrop hosts hundreds of thousands of tourists every year, most looking for winter sports activities, hiking, riding, kayaking, and canoeing. The town does play on the western connection though, with many of the buildings displaying cowboy décor, and the bar claiming the title of the oldest legal saloon in the state.

We pulled into Sun Mountain Lodge just in time for dinner and had a wonderful meal in a restaurant designed to hang out over the valley. The view was exquisite.

The lodge is also promoted as a destination wedding venue and the weekend we stopped in there were several big ones underway. The staff had set up chairs outside next to the pool and the bridge and groom were to say their vows under a lacy white canopy. Just ten minutes before the ceremony was to start, the clouds opened up and the rain started falling. Every staff member in the resort and quite a few of the guests grabbed chairs and carried them indoors to the lobby area, where they set up and performed the wedding while the rain poured down outside.

The next day skies were clear and blue; the second wedding ceremony went off with no furniture-moving required. We peeked at them from inside the lobby but I couldn't help but notice the other guests who were in the pool and hot tub, watching with interest. I don't know, somehow it would seem odd to me to have a large, half-naked stranger standing in the hot tub watching the wedding, but maybe I'm just too shy.

I had directed us off the Interstate in Washington, almost exactly diagonally, across a map, from the first state featured in this book, looking for an exceptional twisty-road ride. I found it, and now I'm looking for more ideas on the best places to go off the Interstate in the U.S.

The road trip never ends.

PLAYLIST

34 songs, 2 hours 10 minutes. You can duplicate this playlist and you can find it on Spotify—USAOfftheInterstate.RumbleStripBooks.DJG Please follow, if you enjoy it.

Sweet Home Alabama	Lynyrd Skynyrd
North to Alaska	Johnny Horton
Arizona	Mark Lindsey
(By the time I get to) Phoenix	Glenn Campbell
California Dreamin'	The Mamas & the Papas
Connecticut Snow	David Stephens
Trying to Reason with Hurricane Season	Jimmy Buffet
Georgia on my Mind	Ray Charles
Walking Back to Georgia	Jim Croce
Idaho	King Harvest
Indiana Wants Me	R. Dean Taylor
Bowling Green	The Everly Brothers
Baton Rouge	Amos Garrettt
Maine	The Tragic Thrills
Massachusetts	The Bee Gees
Highway 61 Revisited	Bob Dylan
New Hampshire Hornpipe	Dave Grusin

New Mexico	Johnny Cash
Theme from *New York, New York*	Frank Sinatra
Ohio	Andrew McMahon
Rhode Island is Famous for You	Blossom Dearie
Southern State of Mind	Darius Rucker
Texas Time	Keith Urban
Tennessee Whiskey	Chris Stapleton
Walkin' in Memphis	Marc Cohn
Moonlight in Vermont	Frank Sinatra
Virginia in the Rain	Dave Matthews
Hello Seattle	Owl City
Seattle	Sam Kim
American Pie	Don McLean
Promised Land	Chuck Berry
American Girl	Tom Petty
American Woman	The Guess Who
Young Americans	David Bowie

MY TOP TEN U.S. DRIVES

1. California - State Route One - Santa Barbara to Santa Cruz
2. Florida - The Overseas Highway - through the Florida Keys
3. Oregon - U.S. Route 101
4. Washington - North Cascades Highway
5. Mississippi – Natchez Trace Parkway
6. Arizona - Old Route 66
7. Vermont - Route 108 - Smuggler's Notch
8. Colorado - Gold Belt Scenic Byway
9. Alaska - Seward Highway
10. Virginia - Blue Ridge Parkway

ABOUT THE AUTHOR

Gail Hulnick is also the author of *Rumble Strip Canada 150,* the first in the Rumble Strip Books series. She writes novels, short stories, and screenplays and, wearing other hats, helps to run several businesses.

ABOUT RUMBLE STRIP BOOKS

Rumble Strip Books are published by WindWord Group Publishing & Media, as part of its Sirocco Press imprint. Each of the plans for these travel memoirs features a personal journey over noteworthy roads in an interesting car.

www.ingramcontent.com/pod-product-compliance
Lightning Source LLC
Chambersburg PA
CBHW050201130526
44591CB00034B/1686